When
Death
Means
Life

STANLEY C. BALDWIN

When Death Means Life

Choosing the Way of the Cross

Compliments of
Christian Supply
Portland, Oregon

MULTNOMAH · PRESS

Portland, Oregon 97266

Unless otherwise indicated, all Scripture is from the Holy Bible: New International Version, copyright 1973, 1978, 1984 by the International Bible Society. Used by permission of Zondervan Bible Publishers.

Scripture references marked KJV are taken from the King James Version of the Bible.

Cover design and illustration by Larry Ulmer
Edited by Steve Halliday

WHEN DEATH MEANS LIFE
© 1986 by Stanley C. Baldwin
Portland, Oregon 97266

Printed in the United States of America

Library of Congress Cataloging-in-Publication Data

Baldwin, Stanley C.
  When death means life.

  1. Crosses.   2. Jesus Christ—Crucifixion.   I. Title.
BT453.B35 1986   234   86-12462
ISBN 0-88070-161-7

86 87 88 89 90 91 92 – 10 9 8 7 6 5 4 3 2 1

CONTENTS

PREFACE

Most books about the cross are devotional. So are the songs, poems, and sermons. They encourage us to be awed and humbled because Jesus died for us.

> When I survey the wondrous cross
> On which the Prince of glory died,
> My richest gain I count but loss,
> And pour contempt on all my pride.

We are also encouraged to express our love to the Lord and to worship him in return for all he has done.

> Were the whole realm of nature mine,
> That were a present far too small.
> Love so amazing, so divine,
> Demands my soul, my life, my all.

That's all good. In fact, it is wonderful . . . as far as it goes. But Jesus did not call us to "survey" the cross; he called us to take it up. This book is about the practical implications of the cross in the daily life of the believer.

Some books and sermons do indeed focus on the practical implications on taking up the cross, but most of those talk about only one thing: dying to sin and self. They concentrate on ways to put to death the flesh.

This, again, is valid. But it is such a truncated view. The cross means so much more than that. Its practical implications for how we believe and live are extremely broad.

PREFACE

The cross tells us about:

- the nature of ultimate reality. What is our God like, that the cross should be central to his plan?
- the dimensions of suffering. Does God actually share in our woes? Do we also somehow share the sufferings of Christ?
- the inevitable conflict between us and God and what to do about it. When the time for the cross approached, why was there conflict between the will of God and the desires of Christ even though he was sinless?
- the prime importance of living by a great sense of purpose. We need to run "the race marked out for us" just as Jesus came into the world "for this very purpose," to face the cross.

The cross also tells us:

- how we should pursue righteous ends, by renouncing force in favor of the kind of love that has no blood on its hands except our own.
- how we should use power, which sometimes means abstaining from its use to the point of appearing weak because our "weakness" is redemptive to others.
- what our concept of ourselves should be. We are "bad" enough to require the crucifixion of the Son of God to save us, yet "good" enough in God's sight for him to pay that price.

So much, so much is in the cross. Yet, until now we have hardly begun to explore these things.

This book does not offer the last word on the practical implications of the cross. In too large a measure it is closer to the first word. May many others take up the theme.

Stanley C. Baldwin

INTRODUCTION

"**O**n a hill far away stood an old rugged cross . . ." So begins a much-loved hymn that expresses some beautiful truths about the cross. Not all truths, however. To the degree that it accents the distance between us and the cross—as suggested by the descriptions *far away* and *old* and by use of the past tense *stood*—to that degree it hinders rather than helps us.

The cross is not only distant, it is also every person's near contemporary. It has existed in God since time began. It shaped the life of Christ long before it precipitated his death. The cross is the context in which the Holy Spirit ministers to believers. And it is the panoply under which Jesus' followers are to serve and live.

We live *today* either by the principles of the cross—*by cross purposes*, we might say—or we live at variance with these principles—*at cross purposes* with God.

We are sometimes at cross purposes with God to such a degree that we unintentionally do him disservice. Like Peter did. When Jesus first began telling his disciples about his impending crucifixion, Peter responded, "Perish the thought, Lord! This shall never happen to you!"

It was an honest reaction; Peter certainly meant no harm. But he was out of step with God. He was at cross purposes when he stubbornly insisted *his* way was right. He was wholly ignorant of his enormous error.

Jesus' fierce reply is startling. "Out of my sight, Satan! You are a stumbling block to me; you do not have in mind

9

the things of God, but the things of men" (Matthew 16:23).

It is frightening to think that Christ might say such a thing to us. We are his own, his beloved, his servants. We have sat at his table and basked in his love. But so had Peter. Indeed, the rebuke of Peter comes only a few verses after high praise: "Blessed are you, Simon son of Jonah, for this was not revealed to you by men, but by my Father in heaven" (v. 17).

The very trait for which Peter was at one moment praised—understanding the things of God—he was next rebuked for lacking.

Can one be genuinely taught of God in many things, but still be seriously out of step with the principles of the cross? Peter shows us that we can be. Each of us needs to ask, "Lord, is it me? Am I living at cross purposes to your will in some of my attitudes and actions?"

Where we find ourselves at cross purposes with God, may we be granted the grace to acknowledge it—for to the degree we do not live *by* cross purposes we are frustrating the Lord Jesus Christ.

Peter, who once resisted the message of the cross, later became its staunch advocate: "Rejoice that you participate in the sufferings of Christ" he counseled (1 Peter 4:13).

In the hope and belief that we too can learn to live by cross purposes, this book is written.

PART ONE

What the Cross Prescribes

C H A P T E R
1

LIFE'S
PROPER
FOCUS

The year: 1985
The place: Irian Jaya (formerly, New Guinea)
The situation: A tragedy—tribal warfare among Christians
The cause: Losing focus
The story:

> The Yigi Valley, inhabited by two clans, is tucked away in a rugged mountain range. Wars between the two groups had been going on as long as anyone could remember, and it seemed impossible for them ever to even the score. That is what the wars were about—getting even. "If you kill a member of my clan, I will not be satisfied until I kill one of yours."

> Then missionaries came with the message of Christ, which swept through the many valleys south of the ranges. Although the Yigi Valley resisted longer than most places, eventually many there turned to Christ.

> It seemed that peace had finally come—peace of heart and peace in the valley. Many hundreds were baptized, churches were organized, preachers were trained, and there was great joy. With the same fervor they had fought each other, they now embraced this new talk of love and peace. People could travel everywhere without the constant fear of being ambushed.

But many of these people believed that with the gospel "things" would come. Did not the white people who brought this new way have many possessions? Surely the gospel would bring them prosperity and riches also.

In the long evenings around their smoky fires they talked about all that would happen— maybe not immediately but eventually. They sacrificially built churches and they carefully prepared airstrips so the planes which would bring all the "things" could land there.

Years passed, and some things came in—axes, clothing, chickens, rabbits, and aluminum for church roofs. But some people began to ask, "Where are all the other things? We are still living in our smoky, dirty houses. We still have to work hard to get food for our stomachs. What really is the difference from yesterday?"

They began doubting, complaining, looking to the past. Then it happened. There was a killing, followed by a revenge murder. The people went back to their old hatreds and feuding. The appeals of missionary Adriaan van der Bijl fell on deaf ears. He writes:

Before we left we told the people they had obeyed the Evil One rather than God—and that he would judge them for the blood on their hands. We closed the airstrip as a sign of our disappointment in their actions, and we left, "shaking the dust off our feet," as the Lord commanded us to do with those who are unrepentant.

We are deeply concerned for the many women and children who are the victims of these foolish acts by men in this chauvinistic society. However, until there is total repentance, there is nothing we can do but pray.[1]

Needless suffering has come upon both the innocent and the guilty in the Yigi Valley, and the downward path began when the believers lost their proper focus on the things of God.

They had responded initially to a spiritual message. God offered them forgiveness of sins and eternal life through the death of Christ on the cross. But somehow their focus shifted to other things—the material benefits they hoped to receive. The end was tragedy.

Surely Jesus warned against this very thing in his parable of the seed and the sower. Jesus said that sometimes the good seed of the word falls among thorns, where "the worries of this life, the deceitfulness of wealth and the desires for other things come in and choke the word, making it unfruitful" (Mark 4:19).

In the Yigi Valley, the message that "God wants you to prosper in everything" apparently insinuated itself into the people's minds. In many civilized countries, the same message is sometimes preached from pulpits, printed in books and magazines, and broadcast on the airwaves.

In the Yigi Valley, listening to such a message led people away from the Lord and resulted in a return to old, sinful ways. The same thing can happen in civilized lands. Of course, the civilized secular culture is not characterized by tribal warfare but by materialism and status-seeking. It is to those sins that straying Christians often return.

The cause, however, is the same. People lose the proper focus in life; they are enticed away by their lusts. Something other than the will of God and the cross of Christ becomes central in their lives.

Our Will Versus God's Will?

Because of the great reconciliation effected by Christ on the cross, Christians and God are no longer at odds. It is not true, as some seem to think, that God and his people are in some sort of competition and we must lose if he is to win. No, having been joined to the Lord, we are now one spirit with him (see 1 Corinthians 6:17). We are on the same side. His glorification does not require our humiliation.

I heartily believe in this Great Reconciliation. We need to grasp it, live by it, and revel in it, as I have elsewhere written at length (*Bruised But Not Broken*, Multnomah Press, 1985).

Even at our best, however, we have desires that may run contrary to God's will. This intrinsic conflict would exist even if we were perfect, for we are still individuals with minds and desires of our own. Even our sinless Lord Jesus experienced this kind of tension and conflict when he faced the cross. He prayed, "My Father, if it is possible, may this cup be taken from me." He did not want to go to the cross. But he also prayed, "Yet not as I will, but as You will" (Matthew 26:39).

That prayer of Jesus says it all. The most critical issues of our lives must be decided by the principles that guided Jesus as he approached the cross. Otherwise we will go far astray.

What are these principles?

1. *Acknowledge that you do have personal desires.*

Jesus did not offer to the Father a contentless heart that flippantly said, "Whatever you want is fine with me." No, Jesus definitely wanted to avoid the cross and he never pretended otherwise.

2. *Ask God to grant your desires.*

Jesus not only recoiled from the cross but he also prayed accordingly: "My Father, if it is possible, may this cup be taken from me." Too often we are like the second boy in Jesus' parable of the two sons:

> What do you think? There was a man who had two sons. He went to the first and said, "Son, go and work today in the vineyard." "I will not," he answered, but later he changed his mind and went. Then the father went to the other son and said the same thing. He answered, "I will, sir," but he did not go (Matthew 21:28-30).

Like this second son, we readily agree to do our Father's will. Too readily. We haven't faced the fact of our own desires, nor counted the cost of obedience.

3. Subjugate your own desires to God's will.

When you have honestly faced the strength of your own desire, and only then, you can realistically choose to follow God's will rather than your own. No matter how committed to God you may be, this tension will exist. You will face a cross.

Before that night in Gethsemane, Jesus' entire life had focused upon doing the will of God. Such obedience had not ordinarily been distasteful to him. As he once told the disciples, "My food is to do the will of him who sent me" (John 4:34).

Jesus truly fulfilled the prophetic psalm that says, "Lo, I come: in the volume of the book it is written of me, I delight to do thy will, O my God; yea, thy law is within my heart" (Psalm 40:7-8, KJV).

But enduring the cross was different. Far from being a delight to Jesus, that was a shame, a sorrow, and a horror of great darkness.

In the same way, we who are the Lord's and who love to do his will must face times when our own desires run strongly counter to God's plan for us—times, perhaps, when we wonder why we still live in humble circumstances and have to work hard just to make a living (as the Yigi Valley believers wondered). And much harder times than that perhaps, when we will need to say, even through tears, "Yet not as I will but as you will."

These times when God's will conflicts with our own become the great tests of our faith. We demonstrate whether the focus of our life is truly upon God or on ourselves. We may draw back, Yigi Valley style, to the eternal loss of others as well as ourselves. Or we may, as Jesus did, endure the cross for the joy to follow.

Our Good and God's Glory

Another example of getting one's life out of focus comes to us from an unlikely source—the American movie industry.

The 1985 winner of the Academy Award for best motion picture was *Amadeus*. The film tells a story of the composer

Wolfgang Amadeus Mozart. But it reveals even more about the narrator of the story, one Antonio Salieri.

As a boy, Salieri loved music and earnestly prayed that God would bless him with musical genius, which he promised in turn to use to God's glory.

Salieri did achieve a significant measure of success, becoming court composer to the Austrian emperor. It soon became clear to Salieri, however, that his talent could not compare to the genius of young Mozart, a talent so great as to be manifestly God-given.

Mozart was an earthy, even vulgar fellow, and Salieri took offense that God would remarkably gift someone so inferior morally to himself.

The crisis for Salieri came when he told God that from thenceforth he and God were enemies. To express this enmity against God, Salieri secretly plotted against Mozart, whom he viewed as God's favorite.

In the end, Salieri became a suicidal madman. He said that God had killed Mozart, alluding to the drive for excellence that contributed to Mozart's death at age thirty-five. "But he has kept me alive all these years to torture me," said Salieri as he saw the ever-increasing popularity of Mozart's works and the obscurity of his own.

Where did Salieri go wrong? At the point where he declared himself God's enemy, certainly. But maybe we also need to look a little closer at his boyhood bargaining. "Make me the best musician and I'll glorify you."

That doesn't seem so different from many other bargains with God we hear about:

> "Save my life in this desperate hour, and I will serve you forever."

> "Make me Miss America and I will testify that my real beauty comes from being a believer in Jesus."

> "Let me be a world-class athlete, and I'll tell admiring youngsters everywhere that Jesus is the way."

"Make me prosperous and I will not only give you
a tithe but a full 50 percent. I'll declare that I became wealthy because God was my Partner."

The question we need to ask in all this bargaining is,
"Oh, and what will you do if God does not come through as
you ask?"

Will you then say, "Not as I will but as you will. I will
love and serve you either way"?

Because if you won't, one thing becomes clear. In this
little partnership you are proposing, you come first. God
will get his due so long as he delivers as instructed. If he
doesn't, it's hello Salieri all over again. You are a Yigi Valley
believer whose real focus in life is yourself and not God.

Now, when a person says to God, "I come first, but if
you'll be a good little God and do as I wish, I'll make it
worth your while," that person is in a lot of trouble. There's
a word for such an attitude. It's *idolatry*. And it's idolatry of
the worst sort—worship of self.

God doesn't like idolatry. The first of the Ten Commandments is, "Thou shalt have no other gods before me" (see
Exodus 20:3). Jesus also said that the greatest of all commandments is to love God with all your heart, soul,
strength, and mind.

One reason God hates idolatry is that it's based on
falsehood. It says something else (the idol) is more important than God, who is the giver of life itself. That's a little
bit like saying your window is more important than the sun
or your dinner dishes more important than the food. It's
not only false, but potentially fatal.

The Subtle Danger

Most people never voice the "be a good little God"
speech quoted above. Perhaps it's a pity they don't, because saying it shows clearly where one's priorities lie.
Most people allow the issue to remain clouded. They want
their desires fulfilled but they want God too.

We may imagine no conflict exists between God's will
and our own, especially if we are committed Christians. But

as we have noted, even Jesus had such a conflict when he faced the cross.

Consider also Paul's companions. We can be sure he didn't select his co-workers from the ranks of the halfhearted. Yet Paul wrote concerning one of them: "Demas, because he loved this world, has deserted me and has gone to Thessalonica" (2 Timothy 4:10).

Because he loved this world.

Paul never begrudged Demas or anyone else the use of this world's innocent goods and pleasures. He told the Corinthians, perhaps the most worldly of early Christians, that the world was theirs. They only needed to keep it in proper perspective. The world was theirs and they were Christ's (see 1 Corinthians 3:21-23).

You see, the world does properly belong to us, but we must not belong to it. We belong to Christ.

Demas was, at some point, faced with a choice. Sure, he could have Christ and "this world" at the same time. But they could not both have *him*. In the providence of God, there came a testing time . . . an impending cross . . . a call to choose between what he wanted and what God wanted from him.

Demas failed the test. The world had captured his heart. The truth was he didn't just use the world; he loved it.

What About Us?

We've said the proper focus of life is to love God supremely and to put his will ahead of our own. We've also said there will be points of conflict—God's will and our own do not always coincide.

Some have imagined that they never coincide. They think that to say, "Not my will but thine be done" guarantees they will have to be missionaries or stay single or follow some other perfectly dreadful path.

That's a calumny on God. Do we really think God is so spiteful and cruel that he would design us for marriage (for example) but demand we stay single even though both we and his work would suffer because of it?

Both Jesus and Paul spoke of people being specifically gifted for the single state (see Matthew 19:10-12; 1 Corinthians 7:7-9). God matches people's calling and gifts; he isn't after mismatches.

But Jesus also said there's a cross for us to bear. It's interesting that he spoke about taking up one's cross before the disciples had any idea he would be crucified. Quite early in his ministry, when he was commissioning the twelve, he said, "Anyone who does not take his cross and follow me is not worthy of me" (Matthew 10:38).

Jesus also described the principle of the cross in his very next words: "Whoever finds his life will lose it, and whoever loses his life for my sake will find it" (v. 39).

We must be willing to lose whatever is "life" to us for his sake. Otherwise that thing has become our idol, more important to us than he is.

Holding On To What We Have

Some years ago I worked for a major Christian publisher. After a time I was promoted to a middle management position and began attending executive meetings along with perhaps forty others.

One day we heard a presentation on how to hold our jobs against the competition of those who might come along and excel us. After some discussion, I asked what seemed to me a more basic question. "Why should I try to hold my job against someone more capable? If our object here is to give the Lord the best possible service, shouldn't I step aside and let my job go to the person better able to do it?"

Everybody laughed.

That's how captive the thinking had become to the worldly proposition: "What's good is what's good for me." (I should point out that afterward the vice-president expressed agreement with me, and I have great respect for that company to this day.)

Of course, I wouldn't naturally choose to lose my job to someone who can do it better. But this is exactly the kind of situation, I believe, in which he that will save his life will lose it.

How many pastors go into the ministry to serve and honor and glorify Christ! They take a church to bless it and build it. At some point, however, their ministry gets into trouble. Their tenure is threatened. Some pastors scratch and fight to keep their posts. Why? It's their life and they are not willing to lose it.

Unless a pastor is willing to lose his life for Christ's sake—put his ministry and reputation on the line as expendable—he cannot be objective enough even to see what ought to be done.

To lose one's pastoral position might indeed be like dying. But Jesus said that losing our lives for his sake will mean finding it. The question is whether we believe him. And whether we have our lives in proper focus.

Too often we don't.

Paul once lamented that he had no one but Timothy "who will naturally care for your state. For all seek their own, not the things which are Jesus Christ's" (Philippians 2:20-21 KJV).

It's so easy to miss the distinction Paul makes here. We begin to think that seeking our own *is* seeking the things of Christ. Don't we want to prosper in order to give money to the work of God? Don't we want power in order to exert our influence for good? Don't we want musical genius in order to glorify God with song? Don't we want vibrant good health as a testimony to God's love and in order to serve him energetically? Aren't all of these things perfectly legitimate?

Yes!

Yes to every question if we are also willing to die to every one of these things—willing to lose them all for Christ's sake.

Paul found that too many Christians of his day were not willing to die to their own desires for the sake of Christ. The medieval Beguine sister Hadewijch of Antwerp expressed much the same concern:

> But today, instead of loving God's will, everyone
> loves himself: it is everyone's will to have peace
> and rest, to live with God in riches and might and

> to be one with him in his joy and glory. We all
> want to be God along with God; but God knows
> that there are few of us who want to be man with
> him in his humanity, to carry his cross with him
> . . .[2]

Those words were written hundreds of years ago, but they sound as if they could have been written to describe our day. No doubt in every age it has been more appealing to be God along with God than to be man along with the man Christ Jesus. It has never been easy to lose that which is life to us, even when God clearly calls us to such a path.

Nevertheless, that's how it must be. We must renounce the way of Salieri and the Yigi Valley believers. We must march like Abraham to Mt. Moriah, take the wood and the fire and the knife, and fully intend to sacrifice our Isaac, even though he represents not only the great love of our life but also our best hope for glorifying God.

That's what it means to take up the cross. That's what it means to have life in proper focus.

1. *The Alliance Witness*, Nyack, N.Y., 25 September 1985, pp. 16-17. Used by permission.

2. *Medieval Netherlands Religious Literature*, trans. E. Colledge, (Sythoff, London House, and Heinemann), p. 50.

CHAPTER

2

WHAT IT MEANS TO BE BLESSED

Doug has been on my mind lately. That's quite remarkable since he has been dead for several years. Even more remarkable, I never knew him.

Doug was a distant relative—my brother's wife's sister's son. What did that make him to me? A nephew twice removed? Whatever, so far as I can remember, I never met Doug. But he has been on my mind because of something my sister-in-law Shirley said about him. Something about the meaning he found in his own tragic life and death.

Doug was seventeen when he became ill with what the doctor first thought was appendicitis. Surgery revealed that his body was full of a rare form of cancer, and the doctors just closed him up again, giving no hope for his survival. For three weeks after that, Doug was suicidal and had to be watched day and night.

Then he was transferred to a major university hospital for the second of what turned out to be some twenty operations over the next six years. Several times the doctors doubted that Doug would survive surgery, but each time he pulled through. Barely. No one else had ever lived so long with his disease.

After one difficult surgery, my brother Ron went to see him. Ron thought he was prepared mentally for Doug's condition. Yet when he entered the room and saw the emaciated figure in the bed, Ron's knees literally buckled. Doug weighed sixty-five pounds.

Still, Doug held on. Strangely, he not only began to recover but also to gain an inner strength. Most of his internal organs were gone by now. He knew he could never be a father, never live a normal life, never hold a full-time job. He carried a bag to catch his body wastes. He had to avoid any situation that might expose him to disease against which his body had no defense.

Yet, he almost seemed to glow when he recounted how doctors had already saved the life of one child because of what they had learned from his case. Medical scientists from near and far had come to study his progress.

The last year of Doug's life was the best. He not only went home from the hospital but got a part-time job and a motorcycle. One day when he was riding, a motorist coming the other way turned left in front of him. Doug slammed into the side of the car, breaking both legs and scraping the skin from his thigh. The injuries would have been serious for anyone. For Doug they proved fatal.

His short and tragic life had one redeeming feature so far as Doug himself was concerned. There was meaning in it.

A Principle of the Cross

When Doug chose, at only seventeen years of age, to go on living despite the pain and indignity of his disease, he exemplified a central principle of the cross. He said in effect: "As bad as this is, I have found meaning in it and it's better than the alternative, to seek escape in oblivion."

The cross of Jesus Christ is the pivot and focus of time and eternity, a central reality of all that is, so it embodies many truths. One of the cardinal truths the cross reveals—and Doug's life exemplified—is that *meaning in life is more important than ease.*

This dynamic principle is set forth in Hebrews 12:1-2:

> Therefore, since we are surrounded by such a great cloud of witnesses, let us throw off everything that hinders and the sin that so easily entangles, and let us run with perseverance the race marked out for us. Let us fix our eyes on

Jesus, the author and perfecter of our faith, who for the joy set before him endured the cross, scorning its shame, and sat down at the right hand of the throne of God.

Every phrase of this passage is heavy with truth. The theme of choosing meaning over ease comes through powerfully. We read that there is a "race marked out for us." Life does not consist merely of lolling around on God's green earth, or even of jogging through it. We are designated runners in a great race that we must at all costs win.

Our model for the race is Jesus. Not just Jesus the good man, or Jesus the superb teacher, or Jesus the beloved Son of God, though he is all of those things. Not even just Jesus the Savior of all who put their trust in him, though he is certainly that. But the passage before us calls us to "fix our eyes on Jesus" who "endured the cross." Our model for life's race is Jesus the crucified.

Jesus had a supreme goal and purpose in life, the fulfilling of which was to bring him great joy. Reaching his goal required, however, that he endure the cross. The two went together. "For the joy set before him (he) endured the cross." He could not have the blessing without the cost.

To endure the cross was a horrendous experience for Jesus. It is beyond the power of words to describe. No doubt Jesus shrank from the cross with every fiber of his being. In the Garden of Gethsemane, he sweat what seemed to be great drops of blood while imploring the Father to spare him the ordeal of the cross.

At the same time, Jesus "despised" or scorned the shame of the cross. He counted crucifixion a small sacrifice in light of the joy of fulfilling his purpose.

Jesus approached the cross with both eyes open. He had already made the same choice repeatedly that he made for the final time in the Garden—he chose the meaning and purpose involved in doing the will of God rather than trying to guarantee his own ease and preferences. In other words, he kept life in proper focus, as that focus is described in chapter one of this book.

In the wilderness at the very beginning of his ministry, Jesus was tempted

> -to turn stones into bread
> -to jump from the pinnacle of the temple
> -to bow to Satan in exchange for earthly power

He refused every temptation, then and consistently thereafter, to choose ease or power or self-aggrandizement over the Father's purpose for his life.

So Jesus set his face toward Jerusalem and the cross that he knew awaited him there. And when the time approached, he reaffirmed his choice. "Now is my heart troubled, and what shall I say? 'Father, save me from this hour'? No, it was for this very reason I came to this hour. Father, glorify your name!" (John 12:27).

"*For this very reason I came* . . ." As we have a "race marked out" for us, so Jesus had a "this very reason" for living and dying. And for both Christ and us, the race and the reason involve a cross.

Empty Living

It's important to understand that the cross calls us to live for a divine purpose instead of for ease. The idea persists that one should call blessed those whose needs are abundantly provided and whose sufferings are few.

Wouldn't it be wonderful if we had the means to just enjoy life? To travel, buy what we want, do what we want, have fun?

No, it wouldn't. A bumper sticker I saw the other day suggests the futility of such a life. It said, "Are we having fun yet?" They couldn't tell!

I've seen the glow of delight in the eyes of a child discovering some new wonder, but I also frequently see the emptiness in the eyes of those seeking "fun." I watch the faces of people at fairs and shows and parties. I see tension and futility more often than delight.

Don't get me wrong. I have nothing against a good time. Just as I have nothing against dessert after a meal. I thoroughly enjoy both fun and sweets, especially ice cream with nuts. If you want to treat me, serve me hot fudge on nutty ice cream. But I also know I can't live on dessert. My body cries out for solid food whenever I've had only sweets. In much the same way my soul cries out for something more substantial than pleasure. I hunger for meaning and purpose.

Christ had abundance before he ever left glory. He forsook it all to die miserably on a cross. Obviously, he didn't view ease as the ultimate benefit.

Jesus described as "a fool" a certain rich farmer whose goal was: "Take life easy; eat, drink, and be merry" (Luke 12:13-21).

That farmer was a fool not only because he was going to die that night and meet God unprepared—he'd have been a fool even if he'd lived in luxury for forty more years, as he'd planned. He still would not have been rich toward God, as the passage says, and his life would have been empty.

Heirs of the Rich Fool

We don't have to guess about this. The United States has seen a generation of people like the rich farmer. Oh, they may not have earned their wealth as he did. They are more like heirs of the farmer in that respect. But their goals are like his. They want to eat, drink, and be merry—and not worry about more serious matters. Their cry is, "Let's party!" They are the lost, empty generation of marijuana smokers, boozers, and thrill seekers.

And they die early.

They kill themselves by their lifestyles, if not deliberately, and they die because they have no reason to live.

"Nothing Tastes"

Many people who do not fall into such extreme self-seeking behavior nevertheless suffer a malaise and boredom that takes over the life of any person lacking meaning and purpose. Society is full of good, solid citizens who are desperately trying to escape from boredom.

J. I. Packer puts it this way:

> The world today is full of sufferers from the wasting disease which Albert Camus focused as

Absurdism ("life is a bad joke"), and from the complaint which we may call Marie Antoinette's fever, since she coined the phrase that describes it ("nothing tastes"). These disorders blight the whole of life; everything becomes at once a problem and a bore, because nothing seems worthwhile.[1]

Estelle Ramey, professor of physiology and biophysics at Georgetown University in Washington D.C., says concerning boredom, "It's not considered a disease, but it is, because it causes all kinds of problems. People will go to any length to escape boredom. When you look at society, a lot of what has happened, including wars, has been to escape from boredom."

Isn't that incredible? Wars have come because of boredom? I find that both incredible and completely believable. It's incredible that man would go to such lengths to relieve boredom. Yet it's completely believable, because boredom is such a common and devastating experience.

To understand how bad boredom is, one has only to consider solitary confinement. The prisoner may be given everything he needs in terms of food, water, and shelter. But he is left with nothing to do and no one to talk to; he has only the resources of his own mind. This is one of the worst and most dreaded punishments a prisoner can endure. It is unrelieved boredom.

Yet some people imagine that they want the very conditions which cause boredom. They seek subsistence with minimum effort. They cut themselves off from others to escape the trouble of dealing with unwanted demands. They don't seem to realize that the life they have chosen is virtually a form of solitary confinement.

They are bored, however. Dreadfully, terribly bored. So they seek excitement. Instead of treating the cause of their boredom, they treat only the symptoms. They chase pleasure. But even exotically different desserts get old when the body craves solid food. In the same way, new pleasures soon fade. The bored person finds himself living in a world bereft of all wonders. He is jaded.

The cause of boredom, meanwhile, continues untouched. There is no deep meaning in one's life and activities. There is no cross, no race to run in the will of God, no purpose for which to live and die.

Empty Christians

Many years ago a dynamic young pastor in our city wrote, produced, directed, and starred in a missionary drama. He rented a large public auditorium and presented his play to several full houses.

I attended one performance, and I was impressed. I still remember some of the dramatic high points of the play. In one scene the intrepid missionary shot a poisonous snake that had just bitten the heroine. The gun was real and the shots were loud. Then the missionary sucked the venom from the victim's leg and spit it into the orchestra pit.

Later a friend of mine who knew him told me that the pastor-dramatist wasn't so sure his great effort had been worthwhile. He had commented after the last performance, "Well, I guess it's all over but the shouting." Then he had added pensively, "I guess the shouting is over too."

I think I know how he felt. We wonder sometimes just what our efforts for Christ are accomplishing. If we are "in charge," we may wonder how much our work serves to nourish our own egos instead of God's eternal purposes. If we are not in charge, we may wonder how much of our effort is being lost to petty politics or meaningless routine.

As mentioned earlier, I once worked as an editor at a Christian publishing house. I liked my job. I saw much meaning and purpose in working with capable Christian communicators to publish God's truth. Part of my responsibility, however, was to attend various committee meetings. Some of them were a drag. I saw them more as an interruption of my work than a part of it.

Christianity Today published a cartoon about such meetings that reflected my feelings perfectly. A committee member has been asked to pray as the meeting begins. He prays something like this: "Dear Lord, please grant us the grace to endure the unrelieved boredom of this totally unnecessary meeting."

The point is, we need a sense of meaning and purpose for our lives, both for the whole and for the parts. Without a profound sense of running "the race marked out for us," we become bored, no matter how busy we are or how seemingly blessed.

It seems to me that the Christian who lives for creature comforts, ease, and prosperity, is especially rebuked by this world's wealthy people who aspire to something better than that. Gordon Peter Getty, for example, was once asked if it pleased him to be considered one of the richest men in the United States. He replied, "No, certainly not. I'd rather lapse back into obscurity. But if my music became well-respected, I wouldn't mind becoming well-known for that. The best things in life require effort and study rather than money. You can't buy an education, and education is worth more than a billion dollars."

The Life Truly Blessed

Everybody wants the "abundant life." But unless we come to terms with the cross, we cannot even correctly understand the abundant life, much less experience it.

I admit that's a strong statement, and you have every right to examine the evidence on which it is based. We have been considering some of that evidence. Consider now, as perhaps the premier exhibit, the life of the woman blessed above all others—Mary the mother of Jesus.

When the angel Gabriel first announced to Mary that she would bear a child, he said, "Greetings, you who are highly favored! The Lord is with you" (Luke 1:28).

Later, Mary's cousin Elizabeth said to her, "Blessed are you among women, and blessed is the child you will bear" (v. 42).

Mary responded, "My soul glorifies the Lord, and my spirit rejoices in God my Savior, for he has been mindful of the humble state of his servant. From now on all generations will call me blessed, for the Mighty One has done great things for me" (vv. 46-49).

What could be better?

"Highly favored."
"Blessed . . . among women."

Blessed for all time "from now on."
God doing "great things" for her.

We need to ask exactly what it entailed for Mary to be blessed so markedly.

First, it meant she was suspected by her fiance of being immoral. Joseph thought she had been with another man. Only the direct intervention of God deterred him from rejecting her completely.

We don't know what the other people of Nazareth thought and said and did about the apparent illegitimate pregnancy of Joseph's girlfriend. Knowing Joseph's initial reaction, we can guess. I doubt that the pair would even try to convince the neighbors that Mary was still a virgin and was with child by the Holy Spirit.

In any case, we know that Mary had to take a long, arduous trip to Bethlehem when she was in the last stages of pregnancy. She had to take lodging in a stable and give birth to her first child far from home and loved ones.

This was the beginning of her sorrows. At the dedication of the Child, a devout man named Simeon prophesied of his destiny. Then he said to Mary, as if an afterthought, "A sword will pierce your own soul too" (Luke 2:35).

Thirty-three years later, when Mary stood at the foot of the cross and saw a Roman spear pierce the side of her crucified Son, we may be sure the sword pierced her soul.

Blessed of God?

Highly favored?

Great things?

Not if "blessed" means free from sorrow and difficulty. Not if "favored" means knowing a life of ease and prosperity. Not if "great things" have to do with earthly power and prestige and success.

How, then, was Mary blessed? Ah, she knew the glory of living for a divine purpose, of having transcendent meaning in her life. She, an obscure maiden from the despised town of Nazareth, was the direct agent of Messiah's coming.

I believe everyone wants meaning in life. Still, we would just as soon have it without a sword in our soul.

Without the cross.

Mary couldn't.

Jesus couldn't.

Neither can we, for reasons we shall seek to understand more fully as we continue.

---

1. *Knowing God*, J. I. Packer (Downers Grove, Ill.: InterVarsity Press, 1973), p. 29.

CHAPTER
3

WHAT GOD WANTS FOR US ABOVE ALL ELSE

Jesus died!

He died on a cross.

It was a horrible death.

Yet it was voluntary. Jesus said, "I lay down my life for the sheep. . . . No one takes it from me, but I lay it down of my own accord" (John 10:15-18).

"For the sheep." What did Jesus want for the sheep that was worth laying down his life?

On so crucial a question as Christ's purpose in dying, we must not go astray or deny him the reward of his suffering. The price he paid was too high.

Biblical Answers

Scripture speaks directly to the question we have raised; we are not left to speculate.

1. *God wants to save us from our sins.*

The New Testament bears extensive witness to that fact, and Paul declares it a trustworthy saying that deserves full acceptance: "Christ Jesus came into the world to save sinners" (1 Timothy 1:15). Central to the gospel is the great truth that "Christ died for our sins according to the Scriptures" (1 Corinthians 15:3).

One thing the Lord wants most for us, then, is that we might be saved. Any person who fails to receive Christ as Savior directly opposes this desire of God. Nothing else one does can possibly make up for this omission.

That's why Jesus answered as he did when the crowd asked him, "What must we do to do the work of God?"

He replied, "The work of God is this: to believe in the one he has sent" (John 6:29).

Have you believed in Christ as your Savior from sin?

2. *God wants to transfer the focus of our lives from ourselves to him.*

When we understand that Christ died for our sins, we have grasped one great truth of the cross, but another remains. As Paul put it, "He died for all, that those who live should no longer live for themselves but for him who died for them and was raised again" (2 Corinthians 5:15).

No longer live for themselves, but for him. God's strongest desire for us is that we not only be saved from sin but also live for Christ rather than for ourselves. In Romans 14:9 we read that Christ died "that he might be the Lord of both the dead and the living."

This brings us again to the theme of our first chapter, that the proper focus of life is on doing the will of God and accepting his lordship over our lives, even when doing so conflicts with our own desires.

Are you living by the principle, "Not my will but thine be done"? Is Jesus your Lord?

Is That All There Is?

Some people don't seem happy when I tell them what I've just explained about God's supreme desire for us. They seem disappointed, even bored.

"You mean the best you can tell us about Christianity is that it offers salvation and a life of self-sacrificing service to God?"

Yes. I'm sorry if you are disappointed.

"You're not going to offer us the life abundant, with health, prosperity, status, and all that really good stuff?"

Life abundant, yes. Being saved from sin and living for Christ *is* life abundant.

"But nothing more, huh?"

There is nothing more. There's something else, but it's all small potatoes, just fringe benefits, compared to . . .

"Yeah, we know . . . compared to being saved and living for God."

Well, friend, that's what Jesus taught. He said that having eternal life *is* the really good stuff. Better even than, say, power to cast out demons.

"Oh, yeah, where do you find that?"

It's in Luke, chapter 10. Jesus sent out seventy-two disciples to minister. They returned exclaiming that even the demons submitted to them in Jesus' name. Jesus answered, "Do not rejoice that the spirits submit to you, but rejoice that your names are recorded in heaven" (vv. 17-20).

Salvation—that's the treasure Christ wanted so much to provide for us that he would go to the cross. And that's what he wants us to prize also.

That's why I get bent out of shape about the frequent misapplication of 3 John 2: "I wish above all things that thou mayest prosper and be in health, even as thy soul prospereth" (KJV). Some take this personal greeting of the apostle John to Gaius as an expression of God's supreme will for all of us. I can't do that because I know very well that there are a number of things God is concerned about more than our health and wealth—our salvation and our service to Jesus Christ being two of them.

It's not that I have anything against health and prosperity. Neither am I full of sour grapes because I personally lack these things. I have in fact enjoyed a fair measure of both. I'm willing to grant, too, that a person may be sick or poor as a result of being out-of-step with God. Sometimes that's obvious. The prodigal son is a case in point.

I believe in a God who, as Jesus put it, knows how to give good gifts to those who ask him (see Matthew 7:11). I have no problem with any of that.

But . . . .

We cannot properly claim either health or prosperity as our *right*. We cannot represent them to be a divine *guarantee* to anyone else. And ardently seeking prosperity or encouraging others to do so is wrong in itself. Please consider the biblical record with me.

What's Wrong With It?

Health and prosperity cannot be claimed as a right, simply because the curse has not yet been lifted. Two passages of Scripture make it clear that the redemption provided by Jesus through his death on the cross is not yet fully in effect.

The first such passage is Romans 8:18-25:

> I consider that our present sufferings are not worth comparing with the glory that will be revealed in us. The creation waits in eager expectation for the sons of God to be revealed. For the creation was subjected to frustration, not by its own choice, but by the will of the one who subjected it, in hope that the creation itself will be liberated from its bondage to decay and brought into the glorious freedom of the children of God.
>
> We know that the whole creation has been groaning as in the pains of childbirth right up to the present time. Not only so, but we ourselves, who have the firstfruits of the Spirit, groan inwardly as we wait eagerly for our adoption as sons, the redemption of our bodies. For in this hope we were saved. But hope that is seen is no hope at all. Who hopes for what he already has? But if we hope for what we do not yet have, we wait for it patiently.

Throughout this passage the message comes through that the physical benefits of our redemption are to be experienced fully in the future, not now. Trace the teaching as we chart it:

Verse	What Is Now	What Will Be Hereafter
18	sufferings	glory
19	waiting	revealed as sons
20,21	frustration, hope	liberation, no decay
22,23	groaning, waiting	redemption of body

Verses 24 and 25 sum up by saying that one can hope for something only if one does not already have it. The redemption of the body is not ours yet and will not be until the resurrection, when "we shall be changed . . . then the saying that is written will come true: 'Death has been swallowed up in victory' " (1 Corinthians 15:52,54).

Until the resurrection, the conditions in column one will continue to afflict us. We will know suffering, waiting, frustration, and groaning. All are part of the present. These things are undesirable and reflect a fallen creation. Nevertheless, they can also be useful in building character. Whatever else we say about present trials, either good or bad, we should at least accept reality; this is the way things are.

Living with Reality

Think of that column one problem "frustration" for a moment. I don't know about you, but I get frustrated a lot. Things go wrong almost any time I try to accomplish something. It's the outworking of the original curse: God told Adam the ground he cultivated would not only bring forth the food crops he wanted, but also thorns and thistles he definitely did not want (see Genesis 3:18).

Yesterday I was in my office working by 6:30 A.M. One simple chore soon stymied me. I wanted to mail a complimentary copy of a new book to a friend about whom I had written, but I could not find her address. I had to search and search.

When breakfast time approached, I went out to pick a few fresh raspberries to eat with my shredded wheat—and decided to fill three more small boxes so my wife Marge could make a batch of jelly. Unfortunately, the larger box in which I carried the small ones had a loose flap on one side. When I lifted my fresh-picked harvest by that side of the box, the flap gave way and dumped my berries on the ground.

After breakfast, Marge and I took time for a morning walk . . . but where were my walking shoes? "They have to be somewhere," I muttered as I rummaged through cluttered closet and cluttered memory.

You get the idea.

We live as imperfect people in a fallen world. Sometimes that means we dump a few boxes of raspberries or can't find things. At other times, the situation becomes much more serious.

Last night, while out for dinner, I made a new acquaintance. A lifelong farmer, he had recently lost a valuable hay crop because he cut it right before a heavy rain that the weather forecasters had failed to predict.

When I got home, the 10:00 P.M. news reported that fifteen people had gotten sick, some seriously, from eating striped watermelon contaminated with a pesticide. The news report proceeded to warn listeners about store chains likely to have bad melons.

This morning, the news is worse. Tons of watermelons must be destroyed because some are contaminated. Many innocent watermelon growers (Christians among them, no doubt) will lose a lot of money, and some may be ruined.

Frustration, suffering, waiting, groaning . . . all a part of life on earth. Some people will be relatively prosperous and healthy anyhow. I haven't said you cannot be healthy and prosperous, only that there is no divine guarantee of it, and therefore it cannot be claimed.

Living Grandly

A second passage indicates that believers misunderstand what the abundant life is when they expect kingdom blessings here and now. Christians in the troubled church at Corinth tried to live grandly. Paul contrasted them with himself and the other apostles as follows:

> Already you have all you want! Already you have become rich! You have become kings—and that without us! How I wish that you really had become kings so that we might be kings with you! For it seems to me that God has put us apostles on display at the end of the procession, like men condemned to die in the arena. We have been made a spectacle to the whole universe, to angels as well as to men. We are fools for Christ, but you are so wise in Christ! We are weak, but you are strong! You are honored, we are dishonored! To this very hour we go hungry and thirsty, we are in rags, we are brutally treated, we are

homeless. We work hard with our own hands. When we are cursed, we bless; when we are persecuted, we endure it; when we are slandered, we answer kindly. Up to this moment we have become the scum of the earth, the refuse of the world. I am not writing this to shame you, but to warn you, as my dear children. Even though you have ten thousand guardians in Christ, you do not have many fathers, for in Christ Jesus I became your father through the gospel. Therefore I urge you to imitate me (1 Corinthians 4:8-16).

While Paul went hungry and thirsty for the sake of the gospel, the Christians at Corinth were trying to live like kings. Paul said they should imitate him instead. Paul was referring to the fact, for example, that while establishing the church at Corinth, he earned his own modest subsistence by making tents (see Acts 18:3). He also received meager support from other churches, but he would not take anything from the Corinthians while ministering there (see 2 Corinthians 11:7-9).

Paul's humble tent-making labor for his necessities, and his refusal to take payment for preaching, were later used against Paul by his critics. They implied that he knew what his preaching was worth (nothing), and that he was no true apostle.

The Investor and the Plumber

The Corinthians, in trying to live like kings, were the ones in error. Yet they looked down their noses at Paul. Their error led them into an arrogant disdain of the lowly.

How easily our values become distorted! From biblical times until now, wealthy people have commonly been accorded preferential status. In the church, such things ought not to be.

Scripture is explicit on the subject:

My brothers, as believers in our glorious Lord Jesus Christ, don't show favoritism. Suppose a man comes into your meeting wearing a gold ring and fine clothes, and a poor man in shabby clothes also comes in. If you show special attention to the man wearing fine clothes and say, "Here's a good seat for you," but say to the poor man, "You stand there," or "Sit on the floor by my feet," have you not discriminated among yourselves and become judges with evil thoughts? (James 2:1-4).

The "God wants you prosperous" philosophy contributes directly to preferential treatment of those with means. They are the successes, the favored of God.

Think of two church members we'll call George and Tim. George is independently wealthy. He made a bundle in real estate during the seventies. Now he can live off the interest, and that is exactly what he is doing. His only "work" is in figuring out where to invest his money for the best return, and his financial planner does most of that.

By contrast, Tim makes a modest living by cleaning out plugged sewer lines. Guess who has more status in the church.

Mind you, George's sewer sometimes gets clogged just like everyone else's. When that happens, George has only two choices, practically speaking. He must hire someone else to work on his sewer line or get in and do the unpleasant task himself. So George calls for help. Tim comes and does the work that George can't or won't do, thereby rendering George a big service.

George appreciates the service and he pays for it. Yet he also looks down on Tim and exhibits something of the attitude: "I am favored of God and you are a poor working stiff." At church, many people defer to George but few honor Tim.

Jesus taught that the true measure of one's greatness is in the service one renders to others. It's hard to see how George is serving Tim or anyone else. By contrast, Tim's service is highly beneficial to others, and it is personally costly to him.

Should George get preferred status? Did Jesus say, "Whoever comes out on top in the scramble for money shall be greatest among you"?

Triumphalism

The tendency to claim now the benefits that Scripture holds out to be our hope for the future is called "triumphalism" and "an overrealized eschatology" by author Donald A. Carson. He writes that those caught up in triumphalism "so magnify the many promises of God for health, prosperity, and victory that they reflect little on what the Bible also says about suffering, persecution, steadfastness in defeat, and death. Deeply, if unwittingly, influenced by the materialism around us and by the American ideal of the classic success story, they transfer such models into the church; and ignorant of both church history and the balance of Scripture, they lay themselves open to teachers whose grasp of the biblical gospel is badly skewed."[1]

This was the situation in the Corinthian church. They "were quick to seize every emphasis in Christianity that spoke (or seemed to speak) of spiritual power, of exaltation with Christ, of freedom, of triumph, of victorious Christian living, of leadership, of religious success; but they neglected or suppressed those accents in Christianity that stressed meekness, servanthood, obedience, humility, and the need to follow Christ in his suffering if one is to follow him in his crown. They glimpsed what Christ had done, yet failed to contemplate what remains to be done; they understood that D-day had arrived but mistook it for V-day. They loved Christian triumphalism, but they did not know how to live under the sign of the cross."[2]

For our part, we must renounce such false and distorted notions of the gospel. We still live in a time when, as Scripture says, "The whole world is under the control of the evil one" (1 John 5:19). The kingdom of this world has not yet become the kingdom of our Lord and of his Christ, as someday it will (see Revelation 11:15). Until it does, we are to live as pilgrims on the earth, not as kings.

Poor Relatives

Scripture teaches us, "Keep your lives free from the love of money and be content with what you have" (Hebrews 13:5). It says that a proper attitude on our part should be, "If we have food and clothing, we will be content with that" (1 Timothy 6:8).

In the sense of having our needs met and being content with that, we can be prosperous. One wonders, though, whether there is any way a believer can properly feel actually rich in material goods. Even if you had everything you could possibly want for yourself, some of your close relatives are poor. How can you ignore their need?

My point is this: Scripture says we are to bear one another's burdens (see Galatians 6:2). It also teaches that we are members one of another, and that when one suffers all suffer (1 Corinthians 12:26). If some of your brothers and sisters in Christ are poor and in need (and some certainly are), then you are poor and in need, are you not? If you have such great faith as to prosper materially, why be content with your own interests alone? Why don't you claim and obtain God's material blessing on your whole family of fellow believers?

The Error of Seeking Prosperity

Is ardently seeking prosperity or encouraging others to do so wrong in itself? The apostle Paul had something to say about that. As mentor and guide to Timothy, a young preacher, Paul had to explain how to counsel people in regard to money. The message was not, "Tell them Christ died to save them from the curse of poverty as well as sin; they should seek and claim prosperity."

No, Paul first condemned the idea of using religion as a means to financial gain (1 Timothy 6:5). Then he wrote:

> But godliness with contentment is great gain. For we brought nothing into the world, and we can take nothing out of it. But if we have food and clothing we will be content with that. People who want to get rich fall into temptation and a trap and into many foolish and harmful desires

> that plunge men into ruin and destruction. For the love of money is a root of all kinds of evil. Some people, eager for money, have wandered from the faith and pierced themselves with many griefs.

> But you, man of God, flee from all this, and pursue righteousness, godliness, faith, love, endurance, and gentleness (1 Timothy 6:5-11).

Paul says we should be content with modest means, concentrating our efforts not on making money but on building character. The New Testament abounds with similar admonitions.

Consider a few:

> Since, then, you have been raised with Christ, set your hearts on things above, where Christ is seated at the right hand of God. Set your minds on things above, not on earthly things (Colossians 3:1-2).

> Do not work for food that spoils, but for food that endures to eternal life, which the Son of Man will give you (John 6:27).

> Watch out! Be on your guard against all kinds of greed; a man's life does not consist in the abundance of his possessions (Luke 12:15).

You say God wants me well and prosperous? Fine. I have no objections whatever. I'm sure he is able to give me health and wealth. He has done it for many others, including some so signally lacking in faith as to deny he even exists.

But, no. I am admonished to *seek* these things. I must make them happen by my faith and by my claiming—or by whatever formula is being advocated. So my attention focuses on these things. I am occupied in their pursuit, but it's OK because it's all for God.

But how can I be preoccupied with seeking wealth for God's glory when he specifically said not to pursue wealth, but rather to be content with a modest living?

A Question of the Heart

Jesus said, "Do not store up for yourselves treasures on earth . . . for where your treasure is, there your heart will be also" (Matthew 6:19,21).

Ah, there it is. *Your heart.* So easily the heart is seduced! Yet, even immature Christians, lacking spiritual stability, are sometimes encouraged to seek prosperity and worldly "success."

Jesus taught that such pursuits work against the nurture of his Word in our hearts. The Word becomes unfruitful because "the worries of this life, the deceitfulness of wealth and the desires for other things come in and choke the word" (Mark 4:19).

This problem may be minimized when leaders tell people they must keep God first because their success, health, and prosperity depend on it. Nevertheless, the teaching still orients them in a wrong direction.

Jesus' emphasis was quite different. He continually distinguished between what people ought to prize and what they in fact strive to obtain.

He said, "Do not worry, saying, 'What shall we eat?' or 'What shall we drink?' or 'What shall we wear?' For the pagans run after all these things, and your heavenly Father knows that you need them. But seek first his kingdom and his righteousness, and all these things will be given to you as well" (Matthew 6:31-33).

Incidentals Versus Fundamentals

The problem Jesus addressed when he said to seek first God's kingdom is one that besets human beings continually. We confuse the incidental with the fundamental. Food, drink, clothing—these are incidentals of life. Not that they are unimportant. To the contrary, they are essential. They are, nevertheless, incidental to life's real meaning.

When I was in my early twenties, I heard a radio personality remark, "We all basically seek the same thing in life— the most pleasure with the least pain."

The statement offended me, though I wasn't quite sure

why. I had been captivated by Jesus Christ and had dedicated my life to his service. This maximum-pleasure-with-minimum-pain philosophy certainly didn't fit me, I thought.

Or did it? I had to admit as I reflected on the question that while my methods differed from the world's, some would say my aims didn't. I also sought pleasure. It was just that I took pleasure in serving God as others did in wild living, in seeking status, or whatever. Though I was willing to suffer pain in pursuit of the goals that pleased me, I certainly didn't want any more of it than necessary. In that regard, I was like the others.

So was the statement true after all?

In a remote sense it was. I joined with the psalmist in saying to God, "You will fill me with joy in your presence, with eternal pleasures at your right hand" (Psalm 16:11). Yes, ultimately I wanted the most pleasure with the least pain.

But in the sense of what one should seek day by day, the statement was false. The strong witness within me said it was a philosophy made of straw. I still believe that witness was from the Spirit of God.

It's not that we should reverse the agenda and seek pain over pleasure. Neither pain nor pleasure, whatever the mix, is the proper focus of life. As we said in chapter 1, our focus needs to be on doing the will of God wherever that may lead.

Pleasure and pain, like food, drink, and clothing, are incidental to life. They are not primary goals. They should be viewed more as traveling companions. Certainly pain is not a companion we would ordinarily choose to travel with. Pleasure is much nicer to have along. I suspect, though, we may well be surprised at journey's end to discover which of them helped us more along the way.

In any case, whether invited or not, whether welcome or not, our traveling companions can't be allowed to commandeer the car and take over the itinerary. That's not what God wants for us. The cross witnesses decisively. God's greatest desire for us— the purpose Christ died to accomplish—is that we be saved from sin and then live not for ourselves, or for incidentals, but for him.

1. Donald A. Carson, *From Triumphalism to Maturity* (Grand Rapids: Baker, 1984), p. 52.
2. Ibid., p. 44.

PART TWO

How
the Cross
Operates

4

BLOOD
ON OUR
HANDS

The city bus was not quite full when I boarded it, so I had some choice of where to sit. I spotted an empty seat that fronted on the aisle, dropped there, and relaxed. It was just past 8:00 A.M.

I had already done a fair day's work. Up at 3:30, I had gone to the inner city, delivered about 350 copies of the morning paper, and now was on my way to attend classes at Washington High School, where I was a junior.

On the bus, I dug into an assignment due that day. My seven-day-a-week, early-morning job didn't give me much time for study in the evenings. Or for anything else.

By now every seat on the bus was occupied and many people were standing in the aisle, practically all of them fresh from a good night's sleep and just beginning their day.

A well-dressed middle-aged couple arrived to stand directly in front of where I was seated. I noticed them but kept at my work. Then the well-dressed man stepped lightly on my foot. It was only for a moment and I let it pass as unintentional.

A moment later, he stepped on my foot again, only harder and longer this time. "Sometimes young men tend to forget their manners," he said to the woman.

I went on with my schoolwork. Now the man came down on my foot with all his weight and stayed there.

I said nothing, did nothing.

"Stolid as the ox!" the man said. He continued alternately trying to shame me and intimidate me until a short time later we reached my stop and I got off the bus.

The man would only have had to ask me nicely and I would have given the woman my seat ... even though I doubted she needed it as much as I did.

I cannot speak for everybody, of course, but I can tell you that an appeal gets much better response from me than a demand. I don't like being told what to do.

Between Rebellion and Idolatry

At about this point someone is thinking, What a rebel! Doesn't this guy know that "rebellion is as the sin of witchcraft, and stubbornness is as iniquity and idolatry"? (see 1 Samuel 15:23 KJV).

The answer is yes, I know it. And perhaps I was guilty. It certainly wouldn't be the only time. But whether I was wrong or not, there is involved here a principle of the dignity and autonomy of the individual. We must remember that many of those we view as heroes now were people who refused to bow and scrape to the petty tyrants of their time who tried to bully them.

When Moses was born, the big shot trampling on people's feet was Pharaoh. He said Jewish parents of newborn baby boys were to throw the infants to the crocodiles. Thank God, Moses' parents didn't jump to obey.

In the days of Mordecai, a man named Haman had everybody kowtowing to him. Mordecai declined to do so. It seems he already worshiped the Supreme God, thank you, and he didn't care to substitute a pretender.

A few centuries later, along came Peter and John. They ran afoul of the whole high-priestly clan. The prestigious Sanhedrin officially ordered them to keep quiet about Jesus. Peter and John replied, "Judge for yourselves whether it is right in God's sight to obey you rather than God. For we cannot help speaking about what we have seen and heard" (Acts 4:19-20).

You may be sure that to have the Sanhedrin stepping on their toes was to feel a heavy weight indeed. Nevertheless, Peter and John were not about to yield to coercion. They defied the orders.

We've had those in every age who don't like this talk about obeying God rather than men. They cite Scripture saying the powers that be are ordained of God and argue that to disobey authorities is to disobey God. What they forget is that sometimes the powers that be are out of line, and to obey them would constitute disobedience to God—in a word, idolatry.

Three hundred years ago these authoritarian people pressed an idea called "the divine right of kings." If a man was king, they argued, God had made him king, and he was to be obeyed like God himself. American revolutionaries, among others, didn't see it that way. They said man was endowed by his Creator with certain "unalienable rights" upon which nobody, be he king or anything else, could properly infringe.

In our own day, some have thought that wives are to be in absolute subjection to their husbands. Where this is believed, the mean spirit of Pharaoh, Haman, Caiaphas, and King George III can and does live on in husbands who stomp all over their wives and expect them to grovel in return.

The Way of the Cross

Jesus has shown another way to conduct relationships, including relationships with those under our leadership. Even when we are right, there's a better way to win our case than to throw our weight around. There is the way of the cross . . . the way of self-giving love.

The cross was God reaching out to sinners—reaching out in pain and suffering—to build a bridge, to reconcile those alienated from him. They were flat guilty, these sinners for whom Christ died. They were in rebellion. Yet God did not write them off, did not thrust them away, did not even turn up the pressure to make them repent.

Incredibly, Jesus made allowances for the very ones who crucified him. "Father, forgive them," he prayed, "for they know not what they do." (Luke 23:24 KJV)

This was not an exceptional case. No special ignorance distinguished these sinners from all others. Sinners typically "know not what they do." They are unaware of the true issues and consequences involved in their choices. From the beginning it has been so. Eve was deceived into eating the forbidden fruit.

Ignorance is no excuse for sin, but it is some explanation. Paul expressed the complex mix that makes up our sinful personalities in these words: "We too were foolish, disobedient, deceived, and enslaved by all kinds of passions and pleasures" (Titus 3:3). Note that as sinners we are both disobedient and deceived; we are both perpetrators and victims, both to be blamed and to be pitied.

But at the cross God approaches us as victims to be pitied. Jesus spoke seven times as he was dying. We've noted that he said, "Father, forgive them, for they know not what they do." No corresponding words from Jesus said anything like, "God, judge them because they are wickedly disobedient."

What Kind of Spirit?

The early disciples of Jesus picked up his spirit of love, acceptance, and forgiveness. Peter preached to those actually involved in the crucifixion of Christ. His preaching echoed the Savior's prayer. "Now, brothers, I know that you acted in ignorance, as did your leaders. . . . Repent then and turn to God so that your sins may be wiped out" (Acts 3:17-19).

Stephen, too, was caught up in the love dynamic of the cross. They stoned him to death. As they did so, he cried out, "Lord, do not hold this sin against them" (Acts 7:60).

This spirit, so remarkable in Jesus' disciples, had not always characterized them. When a Samaritan village was less than hospitable to Jesus, James and John asked, "Lord, do you want us to call fire down from heaven to destroy them?"

To this day some Christians entertain the idea that they would do Jesus a favor by inflicting fire from heaven on those who don't treat him right. Only now they call it a nuclear strike.

Jesus then turned and rebuked his disciples. "You do not know what kind of spirit you are of, for the Son of man did not come to destroy men's lives, but to save them" (Luke 9:51-55).

Now, back to the incident on the bus. I'm not claiming that I was a budding hero when I wouldn't yield my seat on the bus; I'm simply saying it's usually a mistake, if not a sin, to try to force our will upon others.

Warn or Threaten?

The less absolute our authority, the less appropriate force is.

No human authority ever exceeded that of a slave-master. His authority was absolute. Slaves were considered mere property, without rights. Yet even in that relationship, the Bible commanded masters to be considerate of their slaves. Use force, pressure, intimidation? No. The master was told he should not even threaten a slave, let alone injure him (see Ephesians 6:9).

The New Testament often tells us to warn wrongdoers, but it never tells us to threaten them. By using one word and avoiding the other, Scripture witnesses to the spirit of the cross: the spirit of love, not force.

When I warn you, it is to make you aware of and to help you avoid an existing danger. "Warn" literally means "put in mind." Warning is an act of love.

When I threaten you, I am the danger. I will hurt you if you don't submit to my wishes. Threatening is an act of hostility. It is also an encroachment on others' personal rights, for in the last analysis all of us have only one master, God.

A Marred Record

We know all this, yet somehow we keep forgetting. We keep slipping into another mentality. We forsake the cross with its dynamic of love and take up a whip or a sword.

The history of the church has been marred again and again because Christians have resorted to force instead of love.

For two hundred years brave men (and even children!) in Europe tried by force to make Palestine a Christian land.

The Crusades, seven in number, lasted from 1095 to 1295, cost thousands of lives, and inflicted untold suffering. A stubborn Islam remained seated.

"Heretics" have been burned at the stake and subjected to all kinds of tortures by a church determined to save their souls. In recent times we have seen abortion clinics go up in smoke as prominent Christian leaders call for "action" against society's evils . . . and some Christians forget they are followers of One more ready to suffer violence than to inflict it.

This is a spirit we are talking about, a spirit of law rather than love. So easily this spirit masquerades as a servant of righteousness. But, alas, we sinners don't wear our "righteousness" well. Somehow it has a way of making us hard, judgmental, even bloody. Somehow we find it easier to injure others than to suffer for them, to deliver blows rather than to receive them.

Such Hatred!

Dr. Ronald Allen, professor of Hebrew Scripture at Western Conservative Baptist Seminary, appeared on a TV open forum produced in Portland, Oregon. The subject under debate was abortion. As is the program policy, participants were about evenly divided on the subject.

One of the chief proponents of abortion-on-demand was the local representative of the National Organization for Women. She set forth her views coolly and courteously.

By contrast, some of those who shared Allen's anti-abortion views were caustic, even downright nasty in their personal attacks on the NOW representative.

When the hour ended, Allen approached the woman. "You know I don't hold the same views you do," he said, "but I am embarrassed by the level of animosity expressed against you. I want to apologize."

The woman began weeping. "Never in my life have I experienced such hatred!" she said.

In telling of the incident, Dr. Allen remarked, "And then I felt like weeping—for shame at what my fellow Christians had done to that woman."

How ironic that those supposedly championing respect for life and urging love for the unborn should demonstrate such cruel disrespect and hatred for another human being!

Not the Same as Approval

When we get into situations like Dr. Allen's, it's easy to become confused. We aren't able to distinguish acceptance of a person from approval of that person's acts or attitudes. We want to stand for righteousness and against evil; that's in the nature of our commitment to God.

But a strange thing happens. We become more militantly "righteous" than God is. He keeps on sustaining the life of the wicked, but we tend to cut them off. He keeps the door open for their return to him, but we tend to slam it shut.

We do this in so many ways. Parents banish their own children; congregations banish their members. This is not to say that we should have no discipline. Love need not be indulgent. We need to show tough love, which usually means letting a wrongdoer face the natural result of wrongdoing, rather than running to rescue him from the consequences of his behavior.

But what about our hearts? Our hearts! The yearning compassion, the love of Christ, grieving over the wayward, is something far different from animosity toward those who have shamed or misused us or the Lord.

The other day I had lunch with my mother, who is now eighty-two years old. "Can you imagine ever disowning one of your children?" I asked her.

"No, I can't," she replied.

I pressed her. "But what if they did something truly terrible? Suppose one committed murder or rape, or you found out he or she was a homosexual? What then?"

"I still wouldn't disown them," she said. "What good would that do?"

Indeed. What good? Yet I know of Christian parents who have all but disowned their homosexual children. They may not have made a formal announcement of it, but they have abandoned them all the same.

Paul, quoting Isaiah, pictures the Lord in a striking image: "All day long I have held out my hands to a disobedient and obstinate people" (Romans 10:21; Isaiah 65:2).

Get the picture? Here is our Lord, sinned against, abused, ignored. Yet he continues all day with outstretched arms, accepting, inviting, pleading with sinners to come.

On the cross our Lord's arms were literally fixed in the stretched-out position, symbolic of that same spirit.

The Blood on Jesus' Hands

The only blood Jesus ever had on his hands was his own—the blood that flowed from the nail wounds of his crucifixion.

It is significant that these same wounds later became the marks of his identification. After the resurrection, Thomas would not believe that Jesus had risen. "Unless I see the nail marks in his hands, and put my fingers where the nails were . . . I will not believe it" (John 20:25).

Our world is still looking for evidence that Christ lives. Neither skeptics nor would-be believers are convinced by bloody-handed Christians who try to impose their views by force, whether physical or psychological. But when people see the prints of the nails in our hands, when they see self-giving love, the effect is sometimes as dramatic as it was on Thomas. When he saw the nail prints, he fell down at Jesus' feet and said, "My Lord and my God!"

How True Faith Works

It's easy and flattering to imagine that the reason we sometimes get carried away and "speak strongly" is that we have such great faith. Do not strong convictions demand expression?

Yes, they do, but Scripture says that faith works by love (see Galatians 5:6). Something other than faith is at work, something far less holy, when our actions or words are inconsistent with love. We might want to check for pride in one of its many subtle forms, pride masquerading as faith. The Author and Finisher of true faith is the loving Christ of the cross.

A boy and his sister were Christmas shopping in a large department store. The boy, who was mildly retarded, accidentally bumped against a display of boxed shirts, scattering them all over the floor.

The clerk had endured just about all he could from demanding shoppers, and this was too much. He confronted the boy. "Pick them up!" he demanded. "Pick up every last one."

The boy looked at him and gave a one-word answer: "No!"

"What do you mean, 'No'? You knocked them over and you are going to pick them up!"

"No!"

About that time the sister intervened. "Let me handle this," she told the exasperated clerk. Putting her arms around the boy, she hugged him for a moment. Then she said quietly, "Come on, Bobby, let's you and me pick them up together, OK?"

In a few minutes the two had all the shirts picked up and stacked neatly once again. The girl turned to the clerk, who was now feeling a bit ashamed of himself. What she said had profound meaning not only for him but for us as well.

"Mister, you've got to love him into doing it."

CHAPTER
5

REIGNING
IN WEAKNESS

Power abused is an ugly thing. Unfortunately, it is also common. I have seen the ugliness firsthand and have learned to hate it.

When I was a teenager, I knew a young man whose pastor abused his power. The pastor was involved in some conflict with another pastor and my friend got caught in the middle.

I don't know what had caused the rift between the two pastors. In any case, the younger one had a mission church and needed help. He invited my friend to teach a class. The older one opposed the idea.

"Obey them that have the rule over you, and submit yourselves," my friend's pastor said (See Hebrews 13:17, KJV). He used that verse like a club to keep everyone in line.

My friend believed God wanted him to teach the class. But the pastor did have Scripture. How could the young man go against the Word of God? He decided to pray about it and to trust God to make it possible for him to teach the class without defying his pastor.

He explained his thinking as follows: "The king's heart is in the hand of the Lord, as the rivers of water: he turneth it whithersoever he will" (Proverbs 21:1, KJV). "If God can turn the king's heart wherever he wishes he can do the same thing with my pastor."

So my friend prayed. He asked his pastor for permission to teach at the mission church and was denied. A few days later he asked again and got another no. He continued asking. Within a couple of weeks, he was pleasd but not surprised to hear his pastor say yes.

But the man still didn't like it. He began tightening the

screws. If my friend continued teaching, he could no longer play on the church basketball team. The members of that team were close buddies and playing with them was something my friend dearly loved, but his choice was clear. He gave up the team.

Then the pastor began warning the others to avoid the young man. He said my friend was under the other pastor's evil influence. He could tell the difference in him after every Sunday morning he spent at the other church. The pastor said my friend came back after each visit *demon possessed*.

The situation progressively worsened until my friend, and eventually many others, had little choice but to leave the church. That situation, and others I have observed over the years, have produced in me a lasting aversion toward pastoral abuse of power.

Failings of Fathers

Parents often abuse their power, too, as I had sad occasion to observe after I and some of my friends became fathers. One friend of mine had a boy who became the worst brat I had ever seen. I thought I knew why the kid was insufferable. His father would tease him relentlessly until the boy would go berserk. Then he would rebuke the child for losing control. It was almost torture.

I saw other abuses too. One father hollered at his kids continually. He was all over them as soon as he stepped in the door after work. Had they done everything he wanted done? Had they avoided doing anything he disapproved? More often than not he would find some delinquency, however trivial, for which to rebuke and punish them.

I also had my own problem with abusing parental power. I would sometimes get exasperated and mistreat my small son. Usually this would happen after I had tried to reprimand him. I would insist he tell me why he had done this or that. He wouldn't answer, and I'd come unglued. "Answer me!" I'd shout, and slap him across the face.

One day God dealt with me very specifically about my offense. I read in the Bible that I also had a Master in heaven, a just Judge who shows no favoritism (see Ephesians 6:9). I had power over my defenseless son and could slap him around if I chose, but there was One who had even greater power over me. He could slap me around, too, and justly so if I kept on abusing my child.

I came out of that experience with a lasting aversion to parental abuse of power.

The System Gone Sour

Years passed. Our nation went to war in Vietnam. Everyone I knew supported the war. What were those dirty Commies trying to pull anyhow? We had to stand up to them.

Slowly, however, a protest movement began. Our cause was not a noble and just one, some said. The war was misguided and unnecessary. "What if they gave a war and no one came?" a bumper sticker asked. "Make love, not war," the hippies cried.

It seemed obvious to me and most other Christians that these anti-establishment voices were subversive, unchristian, and probably satanic.

The protest movement grew, and with it my own glimmering doubts about our leaders. Demonstrators were shot and killed at Kent State. Police clubbed rioters in the streets of Chicago during the Democratic national convention. I tried to remain sanguine about the establishment. I believed our nation could do little wrong.

By that time my son was part of the counterculture. Not a hippie, but one of those long-haired college kids opposed to the war and cynical about our leaders. I saw that he was sometimes hassled by the police for no other reason than his appearance.

Charges of "police brutality" I had once easily dismissed began now to look plausible. Then I witnessed it myself. I saw two policemen rough up a couple of young "punks" for no apparent reason.

Finally, along came Watergate with all its abuses of power: White House enemies lists, political dirty tricks, actual or contemplated misuse of the FBI, the CIA, and the IRS, lying and bribery and cover-up and intimidation. The investigation went on and on, progressively substantiating more and more charges of abuse.

Like millions of other Americans, I came out of that era with an aversion to abuse of power by the establishment. They are weak people, I thought, with the mechanisms of power in their hands but no strength of character.

Weak people can't be trusted with power, I decided; they will misuse it to cover up their weakness.

Power in the Hands of the Strong

Late in the 1970s there emerged upon the world scene a leader as strong in character as many others had been weak. Here was a man of principle, and of piety. He based his views on the sacred scriptures of his faith. Swept into power by a popular movement that even modern arms could not stop, this man set out to establish the government of God in his land.

Alcoholic beverages were outlawed. Loose sexual behavior, from pornography to immodest dress, was banned. Public beaches were divided into two sections, one for men and one for women. Most positions of power were assigned to devout members of the clergy. The Ayatollah Khomeini ruled Iran.

Soon personal liberty vanished and Iran became a pariah among the nations, her soil soaked with the blood of her own people. Not content with killing those who resisted him, Khomeini sent multiplied thousands to their deaths to advance his form of Islam and even to exact personal vengeance on Iraq's president Saddam Hussein, also a Muslim. Khomeini sent his people to die in waves in the war against Iraq, teenage boys clearing minefields with their own bodies. In one war cemetery alone lie buried more than 400,000 "martyrs" for Khomeini.

It turns out that power in the hands of the strong can be a greater horror than it is in the hands of the weak.

Thinking of all this leaves me feeling drained. How can one live in a world cursed with power-mad tyrants such as Hitler, Khomeini, and Cambodia's infamous Pol Pot, and not develop an intense aversion to the concentration of power?

Lord Acton said it long ago: "Power corrupts; absolute power corrupts absolutely."

The Power Debate

When one reviews the ugly record of power abused, it is easy to go beyond lamenting the abuses and to condemn power itself. This is what Charles Reich did in his early seventies bestseller, *The Greening of America*. Reich wrote, "It is not the misuse of power that is the evil; the very existence of power is an evil."[1]

It's easy to think that way. It's also false.

Noted psychiatrist Rollo May in his book *Power and Innocence* makes a good case for power being not only legitimate, but necessary to mental health and wholeness. Playing on Lord Acton's statement, May says that "powerlessness corrupts."[2]

The need for power begins with the infant in its crib, seeking to exert power over its mother by crying. May refers to the often-cited case in Puerto Rico of babies given all the physical sustenance they needed, but no personal attention. These babies withered and died. From lack of love, we have surmised. But May says it was from powerlessness, from no sense of significance, from the fact that nothing they did could make any difference.

May says other provocative things such as:

> We know that a common characteristic of all mental patients is their powerlessness.
>
> [Concerning successful treatment of drug addicts:] All things are used that will recover some sense of power in the addict, which is necessary for his cure.
>
> No human being can exist for long without some sense of his own significance [which sense May defines as the subjective form of power], whether he gets it by shooting a haphazard victim on the street, or by constructive work, or by rebellion, or by psychotic demands in a hospital, or by Walter Mitty fantasies, he must be able to feel this I-count-for-something and be able to live out that felt significance. It is the lack of this

sense of significance, and the struggle for it, that underlies much violence.

[Quoting Edgar Z. Friedenberg:] All weakness tends to corrupt, and impotence corrupts absolutely.[3]

Where Should We Stand?

Despite my own disinclination to assert power, I must admit that I definitely want enough of it to ward off domination by anyone else.

A counselor acquaintance once remarked, "You have a moderately strong need to be in control, don't you?" I readily agreed, having observed this in myself. But the control I seek is over situations, not people, and is part of a defensive rather than an aggressive strategy.

I inwardly describe the matter as follows: "I know you have nothing to fear from me. I have no sinister designs on you or on anything that is yours. For me to control the situation will not harm your interests. I do not know, however, that the same benevolence guides you. If you were in control, you might act to my detriment. Therefore, I am going to control the situation whenever I can."

This mentality exhibits itself in behavior ranging from making sure I have the law on my side to keeping carbon copies of potentially sensitive letters I write.

This penchant for benevolent control, as we might call it, seems to characterize the United States as a nation. The country spends huge sums on arms not because it has designs on any other country, but to be safe from encroachment.

Thinking in the nice, comfortable way I have just outlined, I can feel pretty good about myself. I certainly do not hanker after power over others.

After reading Rollo May, however, I see I am not so indifferent to power over others as I once imagined. I would have claimed I am in no way aggressive, in no way desiring to move into another person's territory. But the fact is that even my writing is intended to do exactly that. I want to change your mind in matters where I think you to be wrong.

More than even just changing your mind, I want to change your life to conform to the truth of God. In my attempt to change you, I am using the most effective means I know. I believe that the pen is mightier than the sword, and it is that might, that power, I am seeking to exert.

Two Kinds of Power

It's time we made clear some definitions. Power as I have used the term has to do with what Webster's *Seventh New Collegiate Dictionary* calls "possession of control, authority, or influence over others."

By contrast, another kind of power is defined as strength, the ability "to exert force or withstand strain, pressure, or attack."

While there may be some overlap in these meanings, we can say that the first form of power is directed outward toward others, while the second is inward and has to do with personal abilities.

I have written about this inward, personal power in *Bruised but Not Broken*. In this chapter we will examine several thorny questions about power directed outward: What exercise of power over others, if any, is appropriate for a Christian? How should this power be exercised? What does the cross of Christ have to teach us on the subject?

I am going to assume we agree with Rollo May that exercising some power over others is appropriate. I have already described my own desire to exert power through writing. Certainly parents properly exercise some power over their children, as do leaders over their people. Our questions revolve around how power is to be exercised and what the cross teaches us in that regard.

A Pattern for Exercising Power

One passage of Scripture directly speaks of power and weakness as they relate to the cross. We read:

> He is not weak in dealing with you but is powerful among you. For to be sure, he was crucified in weakness, yet he lives by God's power. Likewise, we are weak in him, yet by God's power we will live with him to serve you (2 Corinthians 13:3-4).

Note three things about this passage. First, both weakness and power can be seen in Jesus. He does not represent unalloyed power on the one hand or complete weakness on the other, but a combination of the two.

Second, we are to parallel Jesus in this regard. Use of the term *likewise* brings this to our attention. Like Jesus, we are to operate out of both weakness and power. The expression that follows the "likewise" is especially striking: "We are weak in him." One often encounters exhortations to be strong in the Lord. I can't recall ever being admonished to be weak in him. Have we been missing something here?

Third, the weakness of Jesus is epitomized in his crucifixion. That he should die at all was a weakness. Death invaded human experience because of sin. God, by contrast, is immortal. Jesus died because he was a man, weak. The incarnation that made his dying possible involved assuming human weakness from beginning to end. As an infant, it made him dependent on Mary's care and Joseph's provision. It made him hunger in the wilderness, grow weary in his journey through Samaria, and thirst beside Jacob's well.

But the phrase "He was crucified in weakness" implies more than identification with humanity. Jesus was crucified when he did not employ the usual mechanisms of power.

The Weakness of Jesus

Jesus was crucified because he was weak in political power. His enemies had political clout and they used it with a vengeance. They told Pilate, "If you let this man go, you are no friend of Caesar's" (John 19:12). The implication was clear. They could and would make trouble for Pilate if he did not condemn Jesus.

By contrast, Jesus told Pilate that his kingdom was not of this world. He spoke to Pilate about "truth," a concept Pilate scorned. Jesus had no political leverage with Pilate at all.

Jesus also was weak in regard to armed might, or military power. It is often overlooked that, before he made his final commitment to the cross, Jesus did talk about the possibility of resorting to the sword.

He said to the disciples:

> "When I sent you without purse, bag or sandals, did you lack anything?"

> "Nothing," they answered.

> He said to them, "But now if you have a purse, take it, and also a bag; and if you don't have a sword, sell your cloak and buy one. It is written, 'He was numbered with the transgressors,' and I tell you that this must be fulfilled in me. Yes, what is written about me is reaching its fulfill-ment."

> The disciples said, "See, Lord, here are two swords."

> "That is enough," he replied (Luke 22:35-38).

The record shows that right after giving this instruction to his disciples, he settled the matter of going to the cross. He resolved it in prayer to his Father in Gethsemane. Then, before he could even leave the place, his enemies came to arrest him.

> When Jesus' followers saw what was going to happen, they said, "Lord, should we strike with our swords?" And one of them struck the servant of the high priest, cutting off his right ear.

> But Jesus answered, "No more of this!" And he touched the man's ear and healed him (vv. 49-51).

Jesus renounced the use of armed might, but even if he had not, the two swords comprising the disciples' armory were the epitome of weakness—enough to give his enemies an excuse for violence, perhaps, but hardly enough to offer realistic hope against an armed band.

Jesus was weak in yet a third way—in personal physical strength. Although John tells us our Lord was forced to begin the trek to Golgotha with his cross on his own back, Matthew, Mark, and Luke say another was conscripted to

69

carry that cross along the way (see John 19:17; Matthew 27:32; Mark 15:21; Luke 23:26).

We also read that Jesus died after only six hours on the cross (see Mark 15:25 with vv. 34-37). Pilate was surprised to hear that he had died so quickly (see v. 44). Some have survived crucifixion for days.

Various explanations for Jesus' apparent weakness have been put forth, and it is not necessary to conclude that he was weaker than other men. The point is that he was weak as all men are weak; the strongest body is but pliant flesh, fragile nerves, and easily ruptured blood vessels. Jesus was no different.

Weak by Choice

Though the weakness of Jesus was real and not a charade, it was also voluntary. He spoke in unmistakable terms about that: "The reason my Father loves me is that I lay down my life—only to take it up again. No one takes it from me, but I lay it down of my own accord. I have authority to lay it down and authority to take it up again" (John 10:17, 18).

When officers came to arrest him in the garden, Jesus said he could call on the Father, "and he will at once put at my disposal more than twelve legions of angels" (Matthew 26:53). A Roman legion numbered 6,000 men, so twelve legions would equal 72,000, quite an adequate force to handle the hostile crowd.

Jesus was weak because he willingly chose to be weak for the sake of our redemption and in obedience to the will of his Father.

We may be inclined to say that this was not weakness at all. It took incredible strength for Jesus to restrain his powers in obedience to the Father. In fact, this was the supreme test and proof of his strength. It was not at all hard for Jesus to work miracles, to open the eyes of the blind, even to raise the dead. But to submit to the cross—that took strength.

While all of this is fact, it also remains true that he "was crucified in weakness," as Paul declares. In saying that "likewise, we are weak in him," Paul must be talking about voluntary weakness that one chooses out of redemptive love for others and a commitment to do the will of God.

As important as this principle is, we must always balance it with the corresponding truth. Jesus is not weak, nor are we to be, when a situation calls for forceful action. Note the careful balance in Paul's words: "He is not weak in dealing with you, but is powerful among you. For to be sure, he was crucified in weakness, yet he lives by God's power" (2 Corinthians 13:3-4).

We must resist the tendency to deny either the power or the weakness of Christ. And by extension, as his obedient servants we must balance power and weakness in our own lives and ministries.

When To Be Weak

Second Corinthians provides an extended case study on the use of weakness as a means of serving others. One thing it makes clear is that there is a price to pay when we choose weakness, just as there was a cross for Jesus. In Paul's case, the people misinterpreted his weakness and questioned his standing as an apostle.

There were many reasons for this. Paul apparently was not a powerful speaker or a charismatic personality. He himself said, "I came to you in weakness and fear, and with much trembling. My message and my preaching were not with wise and persuasive words, but with a demonstration of the Spirit's power, so that your faith might not rest on men's wisdom, but on God's power" (1 Corinthians 2:3-5).

People did believe in Christ on the basis of Paul's message, but many weren't impressed by the messenger. Some said, "In person he is unimpressive and his speaking amounts to nothing" (2 Corinthians 10:10). Neither did Paul produce glowing publicity pieces about his accomplishments (vv. 12-18). Nor did he command high fees for his services (11:7-8).

More than anything else, however, Paul showed weakness in dealing with the sins and delinquencies of the people. Not that he ignored their sins. His first letter dealt directly with their carnality, party spirit, sexual sin, arrogance, and irreverence. But it was all by way of appeal. Paul claimed apostolic authority to deal forcefully with them, but he seemed enormously reluctant to use his powers.

Instead, the apostle did everything he could to avoid a direct confrontation, including staying away from Corinth when he had otherwise planned a visit. That caused him trouble because his critics said he was so weak-willed he couldn't even make plans and stick with them (see 2 Corinthians 1:15-17, 23-24). Paul declared, "I call God as my witness that it was in order to spare you that I did not return to Corinth" (v. 23).

Why this great reluctance? Why not go to Corinth, knock a few heads together, establish his power, and shape up the troops?

Unless we believe that Paul was mistaken in his dealings with the Corinthians (in which case his epistle represents a misguided attempt at self-justification), we must conclude there are compelling reasons to use great restraint in exercising power. We have already stated that Jesus was weak, as we are to be, when that weakness is redemptive for others and in obedience to the will of God. But what specific considerations call us to weakness?

Compassion

There is so much suffering in the world that it is easy to become hardened. Some think that tough love must also be brutal. The thinking goes, "the Lord disciplines those he loves, and he punishes everyone he accepts as a son" (Hebrews 12:6). So we should knock people around.

But God does not afflict people readily or callously. Jeremiah saw this clearly in connection with the tragic destruction of Jerusalem in 587 B.C. How dreadful that judgment was! In the Book of Lamentations, we read nearly three full chapters of Jeremiah's unrelieved wail. "Is any suffering like my suffering that was inflicted on me, that the LORD brought on me in the day of his fierce anger?" (Lamentations 1:12).

No mere summary of that suffering can give you the picture—you would have to read the full account in Lamentations of a situation so desperate that children starved in the streets and some were cooked and eaten by their own mothers.

Despite all those horrors, Jeremiah says concerning God, "He does not willingly bring affliction or grief to the children of men" (Lamentations 3:33).

What insight Jeremiah had into the character of God! Many Christians today like to think they live under grace in contrast to Old Testament saints who were under law. Yet they show no understanding of the compassion of God as Jeremiah knew it. God *never* brings affliction willingly. He does it unwillingly and because there is no recourse.

In the case of Paul and the Corinthians, it was Paul's God-like compassion that made the apostle want to spare them. This same principle suggests a test for our own use of power. As parents or pastors or public figures or bosses, are we compassionate toward those under us?

This is not to say we shouldn't administer discipline when necessary. We should. Still, the old saying, "This hurts me more than it does you," ought to truly describe us.

Edification

A second reason Paul was reluctant to use his power was that it was more helpful for the Corinthians if he could persuade them to respond willingly.

We need always to keep in mind what our purposes are. Is it a certain kind of behavior we want? Or a certain kind of person?

Actually, it's both. We want people who will behave like Christians out of inner Christian convictions. Unfortunately, people can behave acceptably on the outside while still being far from God in heart. One thing that has a strong tendency to produce this hypocrisy is the application of power. If the screws are turned tight enough, most people will conform outwardly. Only the most strong-willed, the "rebels," will continue to defy raw power.

Do you see what a destructive effect coercive power has? It subjugates the weak and keeps them from becoming people of integrity. It alienates the strong and casts before them a moral stumbling block of awesome proportions. They are wrong almost no matter what course they take. They are wrong if they give up their integrity and they are wrong if they rebel against authority.

There is a third way, a way out for the strong. That is the appeal to higher authority, as when I went to God about my pastor's refusal to let me teach. But why should people have to surmount stumbling blocks we put in their paths? We are supposed to be helping them, not hindering.

Jesus said, "Woe to the world because of the things that cause people to sin! Such things must come, but woe to the man through whom they come!" (Matthew 18:7).

Paul wanted to bless people, not cause them to stumble. He said, "This is why I write these things when I am absent, that when I come I may not have to be harsh in my use of authority—the authority the Lord gave me for building you up, not for tearing you down" (2 Corinthians 13:10).

Paul realized there was no need to use direct power if the people would respond without it. He wrote, humbly, "Not that we lord it over your faith, but we work with you for your joy" (1:24). This is an apostle speaking and he is addressing what was probably the most troubled, delinquent church in the New Testament. It was the strongest of leaders dealing with the weakest of believers. By contrast, few leaders today would claim to be Paul's equal, and few Christians need so much correction as the Corinthians. Yet Paul showed the utmost restraint, while leaders today often leap for the mechanisms of power.

Are such leaders really concerned for the welfare of the flock? Or are they out to protect their own reputation and authority?

If it's for the flock we are concerned, we need to rethink our use of power. We need to evidence something of the spirit of Jerry Cook, if not necessarily all of his views:

> I do not believe in vertical relationships in the church. I do not believe in the emergence of an elite in the church. You see, I have no power over anyone simply by virtue of the fact that I am a pastor. The only way I can function as pastor in anyone's life is if he lets me. If he doesn't want

me to, there is not a thing I can do. I have no power to make anyone bend.

I could threaten people. I could set up a system of political pressure. But as a pastor, I must make it one on one with people.[4]

Authority used directly, whether by a pastor or any other leader, may be necessary as a last resort, and Paul said he would use it. But he would do whatever he could, even to the point of appearing weak, to avoid it.

Jesus our Lord and Savior was crucified in weakness. Paul the great apostle was "likewise" weak in him. They are not bad examples.

They haven't exactly gone down in history as the most ineffective leaders of all time.

---

1. Charles Reich, *The Greening of America: The Coming of a New Consciousness and the Rebirth of a Future* (New York: Random House, 1970).

2. Rollo May, *Power and Innocence* (New York: W.W. Norton, 1972).

3. Ibid., pp. 25, 35, 37, 24.

4. Jerry Cook, *Love, Acceptance, and Forgiveness* (Ventura, Calif.: Regal Books, 1979), p. 49.

PART THREE

What the Cross Reveals about Reality

6

THE CRUCIFIED GOD

I was in a large eastern city conversing with a radio talk show personality. I had been on the air with this woman once before, and now we were preparing to do an interview on another of my books. The woman seemed upset about something and soon offered an explanation for being less genial than she would have liked. "He's done it again!" she said.

"Who has done what?" I asked, hoping to offer a sympathetic ear.

"God!" she said. "Forgive me, but this personal, loving God you like to talk about has screwed up again."

I stared at her, having no idea what she meant. "Haven't you read the papers?" she asked. "Oh, no, I suppose not since you're from out of town." She paused. "Well, last night an older woman and her son, country people from Indiana or somewhere, were driving through our city on the interstate. They ran low on gas and got off the freeway in what, unbeknown to them, was a bad area. A young man on the street offered to show them to a service station. Instead, he took them to a side street where a bunch of animals like himself beat them senseless and took everything they had. They are in the hospital now, and nobody knows whether they are going to recover or not.

"Where was your God? Those people didn't do anything to deserve that kind of treatment. It makes me furious!"

I started to say something about it being hard to understand some things, but that we should not blame God for the sinful acts of godless people.

She had apparently expected a different answer and she interrupted me to reject what she thought I was going to say. "Don't tell me God allows such atrocities so the victims will learn something and become better people. There are surely ways to teach people without beating them senseless! What kind of God would do that?"

"I didn't say any such thing," I replied, inwardly thankful I hadn't and aware that I well might have. "There *is* suffering in the world," I said. "And worse suffering than what you have just described. I don't know how sinful or innocent that woman and her son might have been, but I do know that Jesus, the sinless Son of God, was treated even worse than they were. He was beaten too, you know, then crowned with thorns and nailed to a cross.

" 'Where was God when those travelers were assaulted?' you ask. Well, where was God when his Son, Jesus, was crucified? I'll tell you what I believe. In neither case did God casually observe from a safe distance up in heaven. I believe that God was bearing the pain along with his Son— and along with that mother and her son who were beaten." I paused. "And along with you now."

Obviously, my friend had a poor image of God. She saw him as either responsible for—or at best callous toward— man's suffering. Hans Kung describes such an attitude as follows:

> What sort of God is this, disinterested, above all suffering, who leaves men sitting, struggling, protesting, perishing, or simply being acquiescent and dying in their immense misery? This, for many, is an excuse for atheism.[1]

This concept of a God untouched by human suffering is not my own. I see God as considerably more involved than that. But I also see what a stumbling block to faith it can be to view God as "impassible" or unable to suffer, as the church has officially taught through most of its existence.

This question about God's involvement with man's misery is not always the quibbling of someone looking for an excuse for atheism. It is a genuine problem.

J. Sidlow Baxter, an evangelical preacher of some renown, faced the problem in his own life. The atrocities of World War II and a sense of the pervasive evil in the universe ". . . swept over my mind with a desolating effect, the more so because, Sunday by Sunday, as a Christian minister I had to stand up before large congregations and represent the God who allowed it all."[2]

Baxter spent some time in a "dark and boggy valley of pessimistic groping." Ultimately, he found his answer in the cross, which he came to perceive as "a supercosmic reality preceding all time, outbounding all history, bigger than the world, extensive as the universe; the profoundest, sublimest reality in the heart of 'our Savior-God'!"[3]

God's Part in the Cross

The insight that J. Sidlow Baxter had into the deep significance of the cross is one we all need. To many people the cross refers to but one thing—Jesus' death on Calvary for man's redemption. While this is wondrously true, it is only part of the story, for it omits the deep involvement of God the Father.

Think about it. When Jesus was crucified, what was happening with God the Father? Did he stand aloof from it all up in heaven or did he enter into the suffering of his Son?

If God entered into the suffering of the cross, one wonders how and to what degree he did so. Did God die too?

This question has troubled the minds of thinking Christians from the earliest times of the church. The Arian heresy, which denied the full deity of Christ, was one attempt to resolve the problem. The Arians believed that since God could not possibly die, Christ could not have been God in the full sense of the word.

The liturgy of the church declared otherwise. Recognizing both the full deity of Christ and the paradoxes implicit in his deity were such sayings as: "The Invisible is seen . . . the Impassible suffers . . . the Deathless dies . . . God was killed."[4]

Around A.D. 500 the church was involved in a "theopaschite" (suffering God) controversy. "A new and instantly beloved version of the *Trisagion* 'Holy God, Holy Almighty,

81

Holy Immanuel,' enriched with 'who were crucified for us,' was suppressed by church authorities committed to standard theology, lest the Trinity be taken for the subject of suffering."[5]

One Scripture some use to support the idea that God actually died along with Christ on the cross is 2 Corinthians 5:19 (KJV): "God was in Christ reconciling the world unto himself."

But listen to James Denney, commenting on this passage: "It is safe to say that 'God was in Christ' is a sentence which neither St. Paul nor any other New Testament writer could have conceived: the 'was' and the 'reconciling' must be taken together, and 'in Christ' is practically equivalent to 'through Christ' in the previous verse—God was by means of Christ reconciling the world to himself."[6] With this interpretation, the translators of the New International Version seem to agree. They render the verse: "God was reconciling the world to himself in Christ."

No, God did not die when Jesus was crucified. Jesus' last words make that clear. "Father, into your hands I commit my spirit" (Luke 23:46). These words would hardly make sense if God were expiring right along with Christ.

The New Testament consistently pictures God as continuing in heaven while Christ lay dead in the tomb. And after three days, God raised Christ to life again (see John 20:17; Acts 2:24, 32; 3:15; 4:10; 5:30; 10:40; 13:30; 17:31).

But back to our original question. When Jesus was crucified, what happened to God?

He didn't die. But did he suffer? Did he feel pain or distress of any kind?

An Impassible God? Impossible!

As mentioned earlier, the church has traditionally held to a doctrine called the *impassibility* of God. Impassible means "incapable of suffering or of feeling pain." The term also means incapable of feeling anything, according to Webster's; but it's usually not pushed to that extreme when applied to God. It's a good thing, for one has to wonder what would be left of the concept of a personal God if he couldn't feel anything—love, for example, or joy, or satisfaction. True, he could still have a will, but he would seem to be rather less than his creatures if he were without feelings. Still, can he suffer?

When I think of the eminent theologians who have held to the doctrine of impassibility, I can't easily dismiss it. Augustine, Thomas Aquinas, Calvin, Arminius, Wesley, and many others believed that God cannot suffer. Such a weight of opinion should not be lightly disregarded.

On the other hand, Charles Ohlrich writes, "In contrast to this long-standing tradition, the twentieth century has seen a reaction—indeed, something of a revolt—against the doctrine of impassibility. Literally hundreds of respected Bible scholars, theologians and Christian philosophers have argued vigorously in favor of divine passibility."[7] One writer who argues for passibility is Michael Green, rector of St. Aldate's in Oxford. Writing in *The Empty Cross of Jesus* Green says:

> If God forgives, he must be a suffering God. Christians have often got confused at this point with the impassibility of God. *Pascho*, to suffer, can be used in two senses. One is simply 'to suffer'. That God has always been doing, bound up as he is with suffering humanity. And he reached the nadir of suffering on the cross. The other sense of *pascho* means 'to have something done to you without your consent'. In this sense God is impassible. But suffer he does, and he must.[8]

Why did the earlier theologians see things differently? According to Ohlrich, early Christian theology "was heavily influenced by Greek philosophy.... For the most part, these early theologians simply carried over Plato's argument that the gods are exalted above pleasure and pain and Aristotle's description of God as the first cause, or 'unmoved mover.'"[9]

Obviously, great minds have considered these matters only to come down on different sides. So what shall we conclude? Personally, I have even more difficulty accepting the doctrine of impassibility than I do rejecting it.

Oh, I can conceive of God being always placid and serene, rather above our earthly maelstrom and secure in his heaven. I understand, too, that one purpose of the incarnation is to give us, in the person of Jesus Christ, someone in heaven who can "sympathize with our weaknesses" (Hebrews 4:15). The implication of that Scripture is that God the Father cannot fully sympathize with our weaknesses because he has never known weakness himself. Of this passage, we shall say more later.

But to say that God the Father is untouched by weakness and therefore unable to sympathize with us in that respect is far different from saying he cannot suffer at all. The cross convinces me that he can. And does.

The doctrine of impassibility would require us to believe that while his beloved Son was in agony in Gethsemane, pleading to be spared from the cross, God felt no sorrow, grief, or pain. I can only shake my head in dismay.

The record shows that as Jesus agonized in the garden, "an angel from heaven appeared to him and strengthened him" (Luke 22:43). I choose to believe that only a God who felt his Son's struggle would have sent that angel.

When we consider the crucifixion itself, impassibility seems even more an impossibility. From eternity the triune God had known only perfect communion as Father, Son, and Holy Spirit. At the cross, that communion was broken and the Son cried out to a darkened sky, "My God, my God, why have you forsaken me?"

It is inconceivable to me that this rending of God's very being could be painless for him. No, God must have suffered at the cross.

The Necessary Suffering of God

The concern that leads many to deny that God can suffer also prompts the denial that God is subject to any necessity. Some say that if God is subject to anything, if there are ways he cannot act or things he cannot do, he is no longer the sovereign God. Some principle or situation or more basic reality rules.

This is a legitimate concern, but it is not a legitimate conclusion. The Bible itself speaks of God "that cannot lie" (Hebrews 6:18). In the original, this is one word— *apseudes*, the word for "lie" (*pseudes*) with the negative prefix (*a*)—and literally means, "not lying." Paul here describes God as the "not-lying" God.

We can say, then, that it is necessary for God to abstain from falsehood. Must he do so? Yes, but this is no limitation of his power; it is only a description of his character.

Another form of necessity that doesn't compromise God's omnipotence and sovereignty is the necessity for some measure of consistency. That is, if we are going to talk about God at all, we must make sense. While language itself is finite and unable to encompass all that God is, we must use it if we are to describe him, and we must use it in consistent and comprehensible ways.

An old quibble about God's omnipotence asks, "Can God make a rock so big that he cannot lift it?" Whether one answers yes or no, one comes up with something God can't do. It's easy to construct such "dilemmas" when you get on to it. Can God hide something where he can't find it? Can God make a person of free will choose to do something?

While there are real paradoxes in our concept of God, these particular "inabilities" don't limit God's power. They only illustrate, as C. S. Lewis suggested, that nonsense is nonsense even when one is talking about God.

Jesus had no problem in talking about impossibilities for a God to whom nothing is impossible. He said, "All things are possible with God" (Mark 10:27). Yet in the garden he prayed, "My Father, if it is possible, may this cup be taken from me" (Matthew 26:39). Again he prayed, "If it is not possible for this cup to be taken away unless I drink it, may your will be done" (v. 42).

Jesus went to the cross because it was necessary. Given that he was committed to redeeming man, God could not spare his Son. By the same token, God could not spare himself that dark hour of separation that tore his beloved Son from his bosom. It was impossible.

The Cross and God's Compassion

Scripture speaks of God in this way: "Praise be to the God and Father of our Lord Jesus Christ, the Father of compassion and the God of all comfort" (2 Corinthians 1:3). That seems a simple and straightforward description of God, but it is really a remarkable statement. How can the "wholly other" transcendant Creator be the Father of compassion and the God of comfort? In fact, he cannot apart from the incarnation and the crucifixion.

This is the whole point of the Hebrews passage which states:

> For we do not have a high priest who is unable to sympathize with our weaknesses, but we have one who has been tempted in every way, just as we are—yet was without sin. Let us then approach the throne of grace with confidence, so that we may receive mercy and find grace to help us in our time of need (4:15-16).

Christ, we read, is able to "sympathize" with our weaknesses. The Greek here is *sumoatheo* which derives from *sum*, meaning "with," and *patheo*, meaning "to feel." Literally, to sympathize is to feel with. Jesus can feel with us because he shares our humanity—as God the Father does not.

But since God the Father, not being human, cannot feel with us, how can he be called the "Father of compassion"? Similar in meaning to sympathize, *compassion* comes from the Latin *com* which means "with" and *pascho* which means "to suffer." One might almost say that compassion is the Latin equivalent of the Greek *sympathy*, though *compassion* is a bit stronger. Webster's defines compassion as "sympathetic consciousness of others' distress, together with a desire to alleviate it."

The word translated compassion in 2 Corinthians 1:3 is not a form of *sumpatheo*. It is *oiktirmos*, which is often translated "mercy" and literally means "oh! pity."

The use of this word reminds us that God's mercy does not spring from a detached, general good will toward us. No, he has pangs, feelings, an "oh! pity" attitude toward us.

Furthermore, the same passage calls him the "God of comfort." This latter word is the same one given as a name of the Holy Spirit, the Comforter. It is *paraklete*, which conveys the idea of "one who comes alongside to help." All of this language tells us that we worship an immensely compassionate God.

As our Hebrews passage tells us, however, compassion depends on a sharing of experience. Jesus understands and cares about what we go through because he went through the same hard experiences.

God the Father shares in the life of God the Son. Thus, the Father has also come to understand us fully in our humanity.

Two Kinds of Understanding

There is conceptual knowledge and there is experiential knowledge. God is omniscient. He knows everything conceptually, but he has not experienced everything. This is the point of that often-puzzling Scripture which not coincidentally follows closely after the words about Christ sympathizing with our weaknesses.

> During the days of Jesus' life on earth, he offered up prayers and petitions with loud cries and tears to the one who could save him from death, and he was heard because of his reverent submission. Although he was a son, he learned obedience from what he suffered and, once made perfect, he became the source of eternal salvation for all who obey him (Hebrews 5:7-9).

The passage says that Jesus "learned obedience." The implication of this statement is that the eternal Christ never knew obedience, even as God the Father never knew obedience. Oh, he fully understood the concept, but he never experienced it. There was never anyone for God to obey.

In the days of his life on earth, Christ learned what it meant to obey. The crowning moment of that obedience came when he cried in the Garden, "Nevertheless, not my will but yours be done."

At that time, Jesus suffered in two ways. First, he accepted the incomprehensible agonies implicit in his crucifixion. Second, he accepted the frustrating of his own will. God's will conflicted with what Jesus in his humanity wanted. He learned experientially what obedience is when he suffered the abandonment of his own will in order to do the Father's will.

This learning process is what made him perfect as the source of eternal salvation (v. 9). He not only atoned for our sins—he could have done that as our sinless substitute without experiencing our struggles. But experiencing obedience and suffering was what enabled him to become our compassionate, sympathetic, merciful, and comforting friend.

David Seamands describes what this truth meant for one young woman he counseled. Betty was an unwanted child whose parents had separated when she was only a toddler. As a dedicated Christian woman, Betty still suffered some of the effects of her traumatic childhood.

> She vividly remembered that final day when her father walked out the door and left home. She remembered being in her own little crib bed in the room when it happened; hearing the vicious quarrel and the terrifying moment when he left. It had left an aching malignant core of pain deep within her. It was while we were in the midst of reexperiencing that incident during a time of prayer for the healing of her memories, that the Lord took us right back into that crib.
>
> Jesus can do that, you know, because all time is present with him. He is the One who said, "Before Abraham was, I am" (John 8:58). Our memories are all there before him who is the

Lord of time. During that healing time, Betty uttered a wracking, wrenching cry of pain which had been buried for many years.

I said to her, "Betty, if you could have said something to your father from your crib, at that moment—what would you have said?"

And suddenly the Holy Spirit brought back up into her memory exactly what she had felt in that moment of total desolation. And she cried out, not in the voice of a young adult, but with the sobs of a three-and-a-half-year-old, "Oh, Daddy, please don't leave me!" And all the terror and the pain of that moment came out "with sounds too deep to be uttered."

Later, as we prayed together, it dawned on me that if we were to translate Christ's cry of dereliction from the cross ("My God, my God, why hast thou forsaken me?") into a paraphrase for a child, we couldn't improve on Betty's words: "Daddy, please don't leave me!" And suddenly, I realized that because of what Jesus experienced on that cross, he understands the cries heard so often in our day, the cries of millions of little children, "Daddy," or "Mommy, please don't leave me!" But they do leave. And the Wounded Healer understands those cries and is touched with the feelings of those children.

This was the beginning of a profound healing in Betty's life.[10]

The Cross and the Holy Spirit

Just as the cross involves the Father and the Son, it also involves the Holy Spirit. Jesus called him *the Comforter*, a name fully appreciated only by people of the cross.

The Comforter, as we said earlier, is one who comes alongside to help us in distress; he doesn't shield us from suffering. Jesus didn't call him the Great Anesthetist. He doesn't administer soporifics to deaden our pain. He has good reason not to deaden our pain, for that would deaden the person also.

When we look to the Holy Spirit to shelter us or somehow spare us from life's unpleasant demands, we forget that he is the Spirit of Christ the crucified. He doesn't represent some other ultimate reality. Father, Son, and Holy Spirit are the one God of the cross.

The other day I was talking with a Eugene, Oregon, broadcaster named Carolynn Rudy. She was a victim, she told me, of child abuse. Like Betty, she was left with many scars and a lot of pain. After her conversion to Christ, Carolynn underwent therapy for three years as part of the healing process for this abusive childhood.

"I thought," she said, "that once I got all that garbage cleaned up, everything would be wonderful in my life. Well, as a matter of fact, I have been healed from that holdover from my childhood. But now I have new and unrelated difficulties to face. I finally realized that there is never going to be a time when there's no cross."

Carolynn described what she called a sudden breakthrough of cosmic consciousness. "I thought of the millions of starving children in the world and I realized we are never going to get them all fed. I thought of the abused children and knew that we will never put an end to child abuse. I thought of battered wives and realized we will always have this heartbreak to deal with."

A person who feels the weight of which Carolynn speaks has but few choices—to accept the cross and go on caring, to lash out in anger at God, or to seek escape and forget the whole thing.

To accept the cross and go on caring was Carolynn's choice. To lash out at God in anger was the mistake of my eastern broadcasting friend. To seek escape and forget the whole thing is the continual temptation most of us face.

The whole world groans under the weight of sin and sorrow. The Father, the Son, and the Holy Spirit care. Cross-shunning people don't ... at least, not very much. They would rather go to a show and forget. They would rather pass by on the other side and leave the wounded to lie untended. They keep watching the TV sitcom with its canned laughter while the beggar lies at the doorstep dying. In short, they avoid the cross, all the while smugly standing in judgment of those who, like my eastern friend, cry out in protest at the horror of it all.

The Comforter, resisted by the angry, and unneeded by the anesthetized, is grieved.

God forgive us.

Teach us what it means to be crucified with Christ.

1. Hans Kung, *Does God Exist?* (New York: Doubleday & Co., 1980), p.694.

2. J. Sidlow Baxter, *The Master Theme of the Bible* (Wheaton, Ill.: Tyndale House, 1978), pp. 210-11.

3. Ibid., p. 228.

4. Carl E. Braaton and Robert W. Jenson, eds., *Christian Dogmatics*, vol. 1 (Philadelphia: Fortress Press, 1984), pp. 188-89.

5. Ibid.

6. James Denny, *An Exposition of the Bible* (Hartford, Conn.: S.S. Scranton Co., 1903).

7. Charles Ohlrich, *The Suffering God* (Downers Grove, Ill.: InterVarsity Press, 1982), p.40.

8. Michael Green, *The Empty Cross of Jesus* (Downers Grove, Ill.: InterVarsity Press, 1984), p. 81.

9. Ohlrich, p. 39.

10. David A. Seamands, *Healing for Damaged Emotions* (Wheaton, Ill.: Victor Books, 1981), pp. 140-41.

CHAPTER

7

THE
CRUCIFIED
BELIEVER

Caryl Silverthorne, a nurse on the swing shift, was sitting on her couch wishing she didn't have to go to work. She just felt lazy today. It would be so much easier to stay home and not listen to complaints of cranky patients or care about their pains and fears.

A picture on the wall portrayed Jesus and it reminded Caryl of her Lord. "I love you," she said.

Caryl expected an inner voice to reply in kind. Instead, the words P*salm* 22 came to her. The reference didn't ring a bell in her mind, and she really didn't want to look it up. Her lazy mood was much better suited to some dreamy reverie.

Nevertheless, she picked up her Bible and turned to Psalm 22. She read, "My God, my God, why hast thou forsaken me? Why art thou so far from helping me, and from the words of my roaring?" (v. 1, KJV)

Caryl recognized at once that these were the words Jesus cried out in agony from the cross. He had appropriated the words from this Psalm, which had been written almost one thousand years earlier.

Caryl was chagrined. Here she had hoped for a tender expression of God's love for her and she got this. "What you should have said was 'I love you,'" she mentally told the Lord.

For a little while, Caryl clung to her disappointment. She soon began to realize, however, that the passage was not so irrelevant to her situation as she had first thought. "I expressed my love for you," Jesus seemed to be saying, "by going to the cross."

The truth grew in its force. She had wanted a sweet feeling. Jesus wanted her to take up the cross. For her, that meant being a servant to demanding and unlovely people. It meant paying the price to be a nurse who cared.

A Common Cup

We have considered the prayer of Jesus in the Garden of Gethsemane: "If it is not possible for this cup to be taken away unless I drink it, may your will be done" (Matthew 26:42). We saw that, indeed, it was not possible. Jesus had to go to the cross in order to fulfill his destiny and obey the will of God.

We will see in this chapter that we are summoned to drink of the same cup.

In other words, we cannot embrace the "triumphalism" of which we wrote earlier. We cannot expect to experience unmixed prosperity, health, peace, power, and glory. We are called to share the Savior's cup, to struggle and suffer and serve and wait.

At one point in their discipleship, James and John illustrated, if they did not personify, the triumphalism error. They came to Jesus along with their mother and said:

> "Teacher . . . we want you to do for us whatever we ask."
>
> "What do you want me to do for you?" he asked.
>
> They replied, "Let one of us sit at your right and the other at the left in your glory."
>
> "You don't know what you are asking," Jesus said. "Can you drink the cup I drink or be baptized with the baptism I am baptized with?"
>
> "We can," they answered.
>
> Jesus said to them, "You will drink the cup I drink and be baptized with the baptism I am baptized with. But to sit at my right or left is not for me to grant. These places belong to those for whom they have been prepared" (Mark 10:35-40).

Note those words of Jesus: "You will drink the cup I

drink." We can relate this prophecy to the prayer of Jesus in the garden that if the "cup" could not be taken away he would drink it. The cup he drank was the cross; Jesus said his disciples would drink it too.

Jesus also spoke of a baptism he would yet share with them. His water baptism was then already past, as was theirs, but Jesus looked ahead to a baptism he was yet to undergo. "And how distressed I am until it is completed," he said (see Luke 12:50). The common baptism that Jesus and his disciples were yet to experience was the cross.

So, then, we are to bear a cross as our Lord did. Many cannot accept this. They say, "Jesus suffered for our sins so that we might not have to suffer. Why should there be a cross for us too?"

Yet Jesus himself very early told his followers: "Anyone who does not take his cross and follow me is not worthy of me" (Matthew 10:38).

One Stubborn Fact

M. Scott Peck, in the opening lines of his book, *The Road Less Traveled*, says:

> Life is difficult.
>
> This is a great truth because once we truly see this truth, we transcend it. Once we truly know that life is difficult—once we truly understand and accept it—then life is no longer difficult. Because once it is accepted, the fact that life is difficult no longer matters.
>
> Most do not fully see this truth that life is difficult. Instead they moan more or less incessantly, noisily or subtly, about the enormity of their problems, their burdens, and their difficulties as if life were generally easy, as if life should be easy.[1]

Peck may overstate matters when he says that life is no longer difficult once we understand and accept that it is difficult. He is right, however, when he identifies as a great truth that life is difficult. As we observed in the previous chapter, suffering and pain exist in the universe at a much deeper level than we like to think The one stubborn fact of the cross cannot be accommodated fully in our thinking without coming to that conclusion.

Perhaps you don't care what Peck says or you think his comments needn't apply to Christians. But just listen to what the apostle Peter says—he makes two remarkable statements about life being difficult, and he packs them both into a single passage: "Dear friends, do not be surprised at the painful trial you are suffering, as though something strange were happening to you. But rejoice that you participate in the sufferings of Christ, so that you may be overjoyed when his glory is revealed" (1 Peter 4:12-13).

Remarkable statement number one: Don't consider trials, even severe trials, to be something out of the ordinary or unusual. Sounds a lot like what Peck said, doesn't it?

One wonders how many of us have really heard this admonition, either from Peck or from Peter. When trials come, the almost universal cry is, "Why has this happened to *me*?" We are surprised. We behave as if such trials are not supposed to come our way.

Remarkable statement number two: Our sufferings are an actual participation in the sufferings of Christ.

That's a statement to make one gasp. We're accustomed to hearing that the Lord participates somehow in our suffering—that he understands and cares. Certainly he does. Betty, in the preceding chapter, found that to be a healing truth. But here Peter says something altogether different. Christ is the great Sufferer, and when we suffer we begin to understand and participate with him.

A Healing Team

Scripture says that God "comforts us in all our troubles, so that we can comfort those in any trouble with the comfort we ourselves have received from God. For just as the sufferings of Christ flow over into our lives, so also through Christ our comfort overflows" (2 Corinthians 1:4-5).

"The sufferings of Christ flow over into our lives . . . ." Here again is this idea of Christ's sufferings being experienced by us. And we are told that the process enables us to comfort others.

We saw in the previous chapter that Christ's suffering made him a perfectly understanding and compassionate Savior. Similarly, it is our suffering that equips us to be used of him to help others. Thus together with God we become a healing team for earth's wounded.

Many a Christian has criticized a parent who is heartbroken over a wayward child, until experiencing such pain himself has changed a judgmental attitude into one of compassion. The same may be said for marriage problems, emotional distress, economic loss, even ill health. We can hardly minister with compassion unless we have either experienced the disaster ourselves or been close enough to feel the pain of those who have.

Little can mean so much when we are part of God's healing team. But until we've tasted the suffering, we can't know that.

Showing Compassion

I know how easy it was for me to be judgmental when I hadn't felt the pain of hard experiences. I am also acquainted with what it means to learn compassion from what I have suffered. Some of these experiences are too personal, painful, and present to describe. But I think I can illustrate what I'm talking about.

As a young man I learned how much a small kindness can mean. I was working the night shift, coming home to sleep on an unheated back porch. Climbing in between those icy sheets was a discomfort a hardy young man could handle, and I thought little of it as long as I was well. Then I had some dental extractions followed by complications, lost quite a bit of blood, and got generally run down. One night I was having chills and feeling especially rotten on my way home from work. Some words of Jesus that I had memorized began to run through my mind: "Come to me, all you who are weary and burdened, and I will give you rest" (Matthew 11:28).

I couldn't hold back the tears as my heart cried out to the Lord, "I am weary and burdened, Lord, and cold and sick and just about done in; I need your rest."

I reached home and went to that cold back porch expecting to crawl shivering between those icy sheets. Instead I found a bed warmed by a big old hot water bottle put there by my mother. She had served on God's healing team.

Many years later, when I had a family of my own, our oldest daughter Kathy wanted a horse. I mean she *wanted* a horse, and that's all we heard when her birthday or Christmas came around. This continued for years. When she was twelve our better judgment gave way to our love for our daughter. Since we lived on the outskirts of town, it was legal to keep a horse—and there was an unused field next to our house.

So it was that Dusty came to live in the empty field beside our house. Then winter made itself felt. We lived where winters are comparatively mild, but that year there was one especially cold and nasty spell. Dusty was without shelter. As the wind howled around the house and I lay in my warm bed, I kept thinking of Dusty out in that cold field. "He'll be OK," I told myself, but I couldn't put him out of my mind. At last I took a light and went to check on him. There he stood with his back to the wind, his head down, shivering. I could think of only one thing to do; Dusty spent the night on our patio.

To some the idea that sympathy for a horse has anything to do with spiritual truth in general, or the cross in particular, may seem absurd. I'm not so sure. Scripture says, "A righteous man cares for the needs of his animal, but the kindest acts of the wicked are cruel" (Proverbs 12:10). On general principles, we ought to have compassion even on animals. But I doubt we can have true compassion on man or beast unless we know what it is to suffer ourselves. Suffering won't guarantee we will be compassionate and kind, but it does equip us to be so. It lets us know something of what Christ endured on the cross and it prepares us to be on his healing team.

Fantasy Worlds and Real

One reason we bear a cross, then, is to equip us to have compassion on others. But that is not the only reason. It is plain that people would not need our compassion if they weren't suffering. Instead of teaching us compassion for others through what we suffer, why doesn't God just eliminate the suffering, for both us and others?

To answer that question, let us review what the cross says to us about suffering. Constantly witnessing to the great truth that "life is difficult" (to state it mildly) is the "if it be possible" phrase of Jesus' prayer in the garden. Those words burn in my soul. They reveal that, for Jesus, it was not possible to put aside the bitter cup of Calvary. For God, it was not possible to spare his Son. That in turn means it was not possible for God to spare himself the suffering implicit in the cross. We are not speaking now of some "possibility" of logic or theory, but of reality experienced.

God had to suffer. Neither was God's suffering confined to a single hour or day when miserable men executed a trouble-making teacher from Galilee. The Bible describes Christ as "the Lamb that was slain from the creation of the world" (Revelation 13:8; see also 1 Peter 1:19-20). Although Christ was crucified only once and not repeatedly (see Hebrews 9:26), there is also a perpetuity about the cross—it spans human history.

Go back in time as far as you can to the very dawn of history. Christ was there already as the Lamb slain. Whether he was the Lamb slain even before that, for all eternity, we do not know and cannot say. Perhaps not. There may be significance in connecting the crucifixion with the creation ("the Lamb slain from the creation of the world"). At creation God chose to make man, knowing that this person endowed with freedom of choice would sin—and would need the redemption of the cross.

To apply time concepts to God is difficult, however, since he exists above and apart from time. Some say that all time is present to God. If so, the cross, with all the suffering it entails, is an ever-present reality to God. And if that is not the case, the cross is still an immediate reality to God ever since the time of creation.

It is hard to fully face this reality—that the cross with its suffering is intrinsic to the experience of life on this planet. It is intrinsic at a deep level because it is the shared experience not only of all mankind and the Son of Man but of God the Father himself.

When we are unable to face this reality, as Jesus did face it in the garden, we construct our own fantasy worlds where the "if it be possible let this cup pass" prayers can be answered in a different way. The cup passes and we are spared to emerge into a world much easier to live in.

The only problem is that it is not the real world.

Dead Men Don't Bleed

A story tells of a man who worried his wife when he developed some very strange behavior. One day he soberly announced to her, "I'm dead."

She didn't need to be an acute observer of human nature to suspect something was seriously wrong. She was wise enough to know, however, that she couldn't tell her husband much even when he was normal. So she contrived to get him to their family doctor.

The man told the doctor the same thing he'd told his wife: "I'm dead."

The doctor, also being wise, decided rather than simply to contradict him it would be better to give the man compelling evidence that he was still alive. Calling a medical examiner friend, he arranged for his patient to spend a week observing autopsies. "And please point out to him," said the doctor, "that in no case do these dead bodies bleed."

A week later the patient returned to his family doctor. "And how did it go with the medical examiner," the doctor asked. "Did you learn anything?"

"Oh, yes," said the patient, "I learned that dead men don't bleed."

It was exactly what the doctor wanted to hear. "Give me your wrist," he said.

The patient extended his arm, the doctor took a scalpel, and raked it ever so lightly across the man's wrist. Bright red blood oozed from the cut.

"Now, then," said the doctor, "what does that tell you?"

The patient stared wide-eyed at his wrist for a moment, then remarked, "Look at that! I wouldn't have believed it! Dead men *do* bleed!"

Insanity involves breaking with reality. What is real to the patient no longer corresponds to the objective realities experienced by everyone else. Sometimes such psychotic episodes are triggered by things too painful to face.

Corresponding to this in the spiritual realm is the break with reality that allows some Christians to behave as if the Christian life were a continual feast. It's fine to think positively and to see life's drinking glass as half full rather than as half empty. What's not fine is to see the glass as brim full and running over when it is in fact only half full.

Escapes Good and Bad

There are ways to dodge the pain that is an inescapable part of living in the real world—ways that come short of going insane. One can use drugs such as alcohol, marijuana, cocaine. Immense numbers of people flee to these destructive narcotics.

Other people find escape in work, in pleasure, in sports, in hobbies, in television, in gambling, in sleep, or in religion.

I'm not implying that all of these activities are on an equal plane. Some are destructive in and of themselves. Others are relatively harmless. Some are beneficial and even necessary in moderation—sleep, for example.

What's needed, however, is an acceptance of the cross, to pray like Jesus did: "Not my will but thine be done." When we pray like he did, accepting God's will that includes a cross, we will also know the strengthening and comfort that he knew. God sent an angel to strengthen Jesus. He has sent the Holy Spirit to strengthen us.

Not only do we need to accept the cross for ourselves, but we need to call others to the same thing. We may hesitate to do this. We may fear some will shrink back from following Christ if we tell them there's a cross to bear. But we have no right to change Christ's message.

When Saul was being converted, God sent Ananias to minister to him. Ananias objected that Saul was a persecutor of the church, but the Lord said, "Go! This man is my chosen instrument to carry my name before the Gentiles and their kings and before the people of Israel. I will show him how much he must suffer for my name" (Acts 9:15-16).

We tend to hide from people how much they will suffer; God chooses to show them.

Taking Up the Cross

One preacher (actually, the same one who is now writing this book) used to say, "There is only one cross in Christianity and that is the one on which Jesus died almost two thousand years ago. All this talk about bearing our cross is just that—spiritual-sounding talk. We experience trouble or live with a difficult person or endure some physical affliction, and we say that is our cross. It is no such thing. We bear the cross only when we suffer directly for the sake of the cause of Christ, when we endure persecution as Christians."

That's what I used to say. And while I'm still uncomfortable about people who too glibly claim to be bearing a cross, I realize now that my definition was too restricted.

The principle of the cross, as we have been saying from the very beginning, is the principle of accepting those things in our lives that fulfill the will of God which we would not otherwise choose.

This is by no means a rare phenomenon. We ought to be doing it frequently. Jesus said, "If anyone would come after me, he must deny himself and take up his cross daily and follow me" (Luke 9:23).

My writing sometimes forces me to take up the cross. Wrestling with words and ideas is not always the thing I prefer to do. Some people get the idea that I must write easily since I have published so much over the years. When they ask about it, I frequently reply, "No, I don't especially enjoy writing; I enjoy having written."

For the joy set before me (completing a book, seeing it published, getting positive feedback, and ultimately believing I have served the cause of Christ), I endure the drudgery and discipline that is necessary.

Sometimes taking up the cross may mean putting aside my writing rather than giving it priority. The key is to do the will of God despite personal cost. Unfortunately, we sometimes engage in doing what seems to be the *work* of God without actually doing the *will* of God.

God's Will before God's Work

Maxine Hancock has found time to pursue a far-reaching writing and speaking ministry although she is a busy farm wife in Alberta. Some time ago, Maxine became involved in teaching a woman's Bible class in her home community. It was soon clear that this choice involved a cross.

One young woman came to the class profoundly depressed. She hung her head, kept one hand over her face most of the time, and wore drab clothing. She had been under psychiatric care for about five years.

Having recently asked Jesus into her life, the woman knew she needed the Bible study, but it was all she could do to summon courage to attend. She persuaded her sister to come along as moral support.

The weekly classes had only begun when the woman started calling Maxine and talking a long time on the telephone. "I knew she needed that," recalls Maxine, "but I thought, Lord, how will I ever get my book written?"

One day Maxine was making her bed, mitering the corners and mentally scrambling to get everything done so as to get to her typewriter by 10:45 at the latest. The phone rang. *Oh, no, here we go again*! she thought.

Then the Lord spoke to her heart. "Are you willing to give me the time it will take to heal this girl?"

Maxine said yes, and that winter she spent about two hours a day with her friend. They exercised together, went on walks together, baked, talked, and prayed together. Today her friend is a gifted personal evangelist and teaches her own Bible class.

Maxine had been willing to minister personally to this woman though it infringed significantly on her precious writing time. She had taken up the cross, literally daily, to do the will of God.

A Love That Lets Go

Gay Lewis has a special gift for working with people. It's a gift called love. Over a period of ten years, more than eighty young people lived with Gay and her husband Tom. They stayed for varying amounts of time, from two months to two years, and many of them were loved into life and health in Christ.

It involved no cross for Gay to join with Tom in accepting these young people, but eventually she discovered there was to be a cross in letting them go. She was creating in them a dependency on her, a dependency that was lasting too long and getting in the way of their continued growth.

Gay was dismayed to realize she was unwilling to relinquish her hold on these young people. The knowledge that she could fulfill a need in other people, that they literally depended on her, was heady stuff. It felt good. Removing that relationship hurt.

Gay had to be willing to take up the cross, and ultimately she did. Life has flowed from that death. In her willingness to let go in obedience to Christ, she became free to respond to the next task God had for her. Now Gay and Tom are working at a retreat center near Washington, D.C., with some more people who need lots of love without possessiveness—ranging from drug addicts to members of Congress.

Forward Edge

Joseph Anfuso of Eureka, California, is director of Forward Edge International, an organization dedicated to short-term team ministries around the world.

In 1983, before Forward Edge existed, Joseph was in Guatemala to research and write the story of Efrain Rios Montt, then the new president and a professed Christian. While there, he encountered a small group of Americans doing short-term relief work and evangelism. They were obviously being blessed in the process.

When Joseph got back home, he told a colleague about the team. "More Christians need opportunities like that to step out and serve," said Joseph. "Most of them would probably never be the same again."

"Well, why don't we organize teams and send them out?" his friend said.

The idea seemed ludicrous. Joseph was already up to his neck in work—the book on Rios Montt was still hanging over his head, plus he had a full-time job as editor of a Christian periodical. How could he possibly launch a short-term teams ministry?

But the idea wouldn't go away. Working on his off hours, Joseph organized the first Forward Edge team. In October of 1983, Joseph led the team to Europe to serve at a home for former drug addicts near Florence, Italy.

The results confirmed Joseph's early impressions. Team members came home changed people; it was wonderful!

But there was also a price to pay if Joseph pursued the Forward Edge vision. It could threaten the secure and familiar job by which he supported his family. Furthermore, that job was with a Christian organization he had long served and loved. Wasn't he already doing enough for God? Was he to risk everything in order to involve himself in a ministry that some of his co-workers viewed as a "diversion"? How did he know the new work would even fly?

Joseph didn't decide impetuously. He prayed about it, counseled with others, planned and worked. Over the next months, Forward Edge teams were sent to construct an orphanage in Guatemala, to carry Bibles into China, to share the love and truth of Jesus at events such as the Mardi Gras in New Orleans and the 1984 Summer Olympics in Los Angeles.

In 1985 Joseph made the change definite. His former ministry that he loved, that was life to him, became as a kernel of wheat falling into the ground, and new life is springing forth. (For information on Forward Edge ministry opportunities, write Joseph Anfuso, Box Z, Eureka, California 95501.)

"Because It's Hard"

Recently I was in the studio when broadcast personality Al Sanders was interviewing my friends Mobin and Gladys Khan. The Khans work with an organization called International Outreach Incorporated, and their ministry is to Muslims throughout the United States and in other countries.

During the interview, Sanders asked Mobin why churches in America do not more enthusiastically support ministries such as his. Gladys, who was listening on earphones, formed a one-word answer: "hard." Al picked it up, and drew her into the interview. "It's hard working with Muslims," Gladys explained. "Churches are more ready to support a work that promises dramatic results."

Even though there are over six million Muslims in America—and many of them are more open to the gospel than Muslims in other lands—the fact that the ministry is "hard" means many do not support it.

Of course, the work is hard for Mobin and Gladys too. A native of India and a converted Muslim himself, Mobin has a Ph.D. from the University of Poona, India. There are many things he could be doing that would pay better and be easier than ministering to Muslims. But Mobin has taken up his cross.

These are just a few examples of people I know personally who are taking up the cross to follow Jesus. I don't hold them up as sterling examples; they are fallible human beings just like you and me. That's the point. The crucified believer is not some super-spiritual person who occupies a position so close to God that neither you nor I could ever hope to approach it.

As Jesus said, "If anyone would come after me, he must deny himself and take up his cross daily and follow me. For whoever wants to save his life will lose it, but whoever loses his life for me will save it" (Luke 9:23-24).

---

1. M. Scott Peck, *The Road Less Traveled* (New York: Simon & Schuster, 1980), p. 15.

PART FOUR

How the Cross Liberates

CHAPTER

8

GOODBYE SELF-LOVE AND SELF-HATE

We hear it so often, especially when the subject is the cross in the life of the believer. The self is bad. We must die to self if we are ever to become the Christians that we ought to be.

This teaching is supported by appeal to Scripture. Paul wrote, "I have been crucified with Christ and I no longer live, but Christ lives in me" (Galatians 2:20). We also read that Jesus told his followers, "If anyone comes to me and does not hate . . . even his own life—he cannot be my disciple" (Luke 14:26).

One spokesman for this "crucified life" of self-renunciation was L. E. Maxwell, late principal of Prairie Bible Institute in Alberta, Canada. In his "Moody Classic" entitled *Born Crucified*, first published in 1945, Maxwell wrote:

> Such a denial of self is no mere severing of this or that indulgence, but putting the axe of the cross to the very root of the tree of self. God says, Cut the tree down, not merely trim it back. All self-righteousness, self-esteem, self-vindication, self-glory, and fatal self-pity—these and ten thousand other manifestations are but the fleshly foliage, the myriad branchings of that deeply rooted tree of self.[1]

In his preface to the book, Maxwell wrote, "Those who read these pages may conclude . . . that the writer 'seems spoiled for everything but to see people die.' We are guilty, verily guilty."

The Self Rehabilitated

In recent years a much different message has come from evangelical pulpits and books. Vast numbers of Christians have embraced what seems an opposite concept to self-renunciation. They openly encourage self-love.

One of the better known among many spokesmen for self-love is Robert H. Schuller. In his 1982 book *Self-Esteem: The New Reformation*, Schuller reports on a Gallup poll he commissioned. The poll "conclusively demonstrated" that people with strong self-esteem are far more

    productive,
    moral,
    socially responsible,
    generous,
    successful in interpersonal relationships

than are others. They are also less likely to be suicidal or addicted to drugs.

Schuller comments, "Unfortunately the poll makes undeniably clear that the churches do not contribute to the self-esteem of persons." He went on to say that only 35 percent of Protestants interviewed and 39 percent of Catholics demonstrated strong self-esteem.

The entire thrust of Schuller's book is that the church today needs a new reformation, one that will make it a champion of self-esteem. He goes so far as to define sin as "any act or thought that robs myself or another human being of his or her self-esteem."[2]

Where Lies the Truth?

L. E. Maxwell, as we saw, included self-esteem as one of "the myriad branchings" of the tree of self, which tree is to be axed at its roots by the cross. Schuller says that teaching such as Maxwell's is itself sinful because it robs people of self-esteem. Thus, one man's sin becomes another's virtue, and vice versa.

Each view represents a position earnestly advocated among evangelicals today. But a significant number of evangelicals, if not most of us, seek some middle ground, not because it is middle ground but because it is right. We see some validity, and some potentially harmful excesses, in both views.

Our task, if we take this moderate position in the self-esteem controversy, is in some ways difficult. As Maria Tolar, one of those who helps me by critiquing my work, says, "It is hard to sound a great clarion call to the middle of the road."

By its very nature, the middle of the road tends to be unexciting. Moderates seldom produce the fervor in others that extremists do.

I can only acknowledge that fact and pray that the reader will recognize the danger represented by extremes in this as in most matters. However dynamic an extreme view may be, and however truthful its claims may appear to be, we must guard against being swept away.

Self-esteem teachings do seem a reaction (and long overdue at that) to the extreme anti-self teachings of the past. Unfortunately, the reaction tends to rush to an opposite extreme.

The Witness of the Cross

The cross resolves the self-esteem question by bringing into sharp focus two complementary truths about each of us.

1.) We must be immensely valued by God for him to redeem us at so great a cost as the crucifixion of Jesus Christ.

2.) We must be desperately needy and deficient if nothing short of the crucifixion of Christ could avail for our salvation.

In other words, the cross eloquently declares both how good and how bad we are. But these words *good* and *bad* are too often used imprecisely. People proceed to argue hotly over them, never having clarified what they mean.

We Are Very Good

When conducting seminars or group studies of our proper self-concept, I often invite the participants to complete the following statement: Underneath everything else, when you get down to the real me, you'll find a person who is _____.

I say, "Assuming no one else could ever know what you wrote, how would you complete the statement?

"Perhaps the assignment boggles your mind. There are so many things you might say. But notice, I am asking you to get to the most basic level: underneath everything else.

"Try to be objective. If people knew you through and through, how would they complete the statement? What would the all-knowing God say about you?"

After allowing a few moments to fill in the blank, I direct attention to Genesis 1:27, "So God created man in his own image." I also cite Genesis 1:31, "And God saw all that he had made and it was very good."

What would the all-knowing God say about you? This is what he did say.

I suggest on the basis of these verses that the statement ought properly to read: Underneath everything else, when you get down to the real me, you'll find a person who is made in the image of God and who is very good. True, the human race has fallen since those words were spoken, but the divine likeness has not been obliterated (see James 3:9). Though the divine image is obscured by layers of sin and debris, it is still there. As the late Francis Schaeffer said, "Man may be fallen, but he is not just junk."

Surely the cross supports this view of humanity. Jesus did not suffer and die in order to redeem a being that he viewed as intrinsically worthless. Isaiah, speaking prophetically of the suffering Messiah, said, "He shall see of the travail of his soul, and shall be satisfied . . ." (53:11, KJV). The travail of the cross was great; in fact, indescribable. Yet the fruit of that travail, our redemption, was so important to Christ that he deemed it fully worth the cost. What an awesome tribute to our value!

We Are Very Bad

As surely as Genesis 1 declares us to be in God's image and very good, Romans 3 declares that we are very bad: "There is no one righteous, not even one; there is no one who understands, no one who searches for God. All have turned away and together become worthless. There is no one who does good, not even one" (vv.10, 12).

Does the Scripture, then, contradict itself by telling us we are both very good and very bad? Not at all. We simply need to be faithful to all that the Scripture declares. We are very good in terms of our worth and value as the supreme creation of God. We are very bad in terms of our fallen condition, which may be summarized as alienation from the God who made us. This is an alienation essentially revolving around self-centeredness. The self is not evil, for God made it and pronounced it good. Since we are created beings, however, it is a terrible distortion when we assume a posture of independence, arrogating to ourselves the central position that appropriately belongs only to God.

More Glory

How glorious is the cross! As we saw in chapters 1-3, it resolves the wealth/poverty controversy by pointing us in another direction altogether. Wealth and poverty, far from being the right answers to life, are not even the right questions. The cross focuses our attention where it belongs— on issues more fundamental to life. Our assets or lack of them are only incidentals, even when they are essential incidentals.

We see that the cross also resolves the self-love/self-hate controversy. This time we are not pointed entirely away from both aspects of the controversy, but toward both sides. We must hold the two aspects of truth—man's goodness and badness—in dynamic tension, even as both are revealed by the cross.

Sane Self-Evaluation

Scripture specifically states the need to balance our self concept. "Do not think of yourself more highly than you ought, but rather think of yourself with sober judgment" (Romans 12:3). Thinking of ourselves too highly is pride. Thinking of ourselves too much is narcissism. Some have called our time an age of narcissism. We are, they say, entirely too wrapped up in ourselves.

The term *narcissism* comes from the Greek mythological story of Narcissus, a handsome young man. Many maidens fell in love with him. One named Echo loved him so much that she pined away until nothing was left of her but a voice. Unfortunately, Narcissus loved no one but himself. Having seen his face reflected in a pool, he fell in love with himself and pined away until he died.

Reacting against a narcissistic preoccupation with self, some have urged self-forgetfulness. Eugenia Price, a well-known author, wrote a book entitled *Leave Yourself Alone*. This plea against the "paralysis of analysis" sounds like an appeal for self-forgetfulness, though the book doesn't take quite that strong a position.[3]

In any case, the biblical answer to self-obsession is not self-forgetfulness. True, we are warned not to think of ourselves "more highly" than we ought. The passage does not, however, go on to say, "but forget yourselves altogether" or "but don't think of yourselves at all." Instead, it says, "but rather think of yourself with sober judgment."

A Correct Psychology

When Scripture tells us to think of ourselves with sober judgment, it is, in effect, calling us to a correct psychology. As much as we may hate the pernicious influence of anti-God psychology, we must not reject, outright, the study of psychology. The word *psychology* derives from *psyche*, meaning "the soul or mind," and *logos*, which means "word." We need a correct psychology, which is to say a correct word about the soul, the mind, the inner self.

We can compare psychology with theology in this regard. Theology is, literally, "a word about God." Some people are impatient with both theology and psychology, and not without reason. Each can be erroneous. Each can be misused.

But as beings who are conscious of the God question, we must inescapably have some theology, some word or concept about God. Our options are not either to have or not have a theology. No, our options are to have a theology that is closer to the truth about God, or one that is more distant from that truth.

GOODBYE SELF-LOVE AND SELF-HATE

In the same way, as self-conscious beings we must have some word, some concept about ourselves. The options aren't to have or not have a psychology. The options are to have a psychology that is closer to the truth, or one that is more distant from the truth about ourselves.

(A full discussion of proper self-concept is beyond the range of this book. For a treatment of that subject, I suggest my book entitled A *True View of You*, Regal Books, 1982. You may also wish to read *The Majesty of Man* by Ronald B. Allen, Multnomah Press, 1984.)

Liberated by the Cross

Not only do evangelicals hold widely divergent views on self-esteem, but this is reflected in an unfortunate polarization of the churches over this issue. Some choose to emphasize our worth almost exclusively, while others focus on our sinfulness. Each "side" thus tends to get hung up on one particular insight into the human condition and to oppose the truth represented by the other side. Much damage results.

Focusing on the bad—on our sinfulness—can contribute to such self-hate as to nearly drown the soul in misery and woe. Oh, the people I meet who are suffering the agonies of self-reproach!

On the other hand, those enamored with self-love can become careless, self-indulgent, and arrogant.

The cross balances these two concepts. When I fall into self-reproach and feel like, "I should just eat a fuzzy worm and die because I'm no good anyhow and nobody would even care if I disappeared completely," the cross declares it is not so. Jesus cares. He wants me to share his eternal glory. He bore the agonies of crucifixion so that I could be with him forever.

Some day I am going to be presented faultless before the presence of his glory with exceeding joy, according to Jude 24. Jesus is not going to sneak me in some back door of heaven. I am going to be presented formally. And do you know how Jesus will feel when he presents me to the Father? Exceedingly joyful!

115

I may not amount to much in the eyes of some. They may not include me in their plans. That's all right, because Jesus included me in his plans. The cross tells me I'm important to him.

But I have also been known to get complacent. A bit smug. Not without reason do the Scriptures warn me against thinking too highly of myself.

When I do so, when I begin to think that everything about me is quite lovely and even my sins are only cute little flaws in my wonderful, endearing personality, the cross confronts me with the true nature of my iniquity. At the cross, he who had no sin was made to be sin *for me*, and there was nothing cute about it. Men reviled him, mocked him, spat on him, stripped him naked, beat, battered, tortured, and finally killed him.

Oh, I've seen glimpses of sin's ugliness in other settings—the drunk lying in his vomit, the child bruised and battered by its own parents, the cursing, screaming married couple assaulting one another, the parents devastated and prematurely aged by a child captive to Satan.

But I don't dwell on such scenes. Something in me wants to put them out of sight and out of mind. My entire culture joins in a conspiracy to hide the ugliness of sin. The mortician either does wonders with the bodies of sin's victims, or the casket remains closed. We send flowers, dress in our best clothes, listen to soft music and a few pleasant words, and then go home to watch TV.

We're insulated. We are seldom faced with the full, ugly consequences of others' sins, and we are even less ready to confront our own.

I'm not suggesting we should focus on the ugliness in ourselves and others. I am suggesting, however, that we should never forget that it exists. There is sin. And sin scatters death and suffering and wreckage all across the landscape.

The cross forever stands as Exhibit Number One of the reality and horror of sin. There, Jesus Christ my Lord was made to be sin for me. When I see the cross, I see how vile

I can be—and have been. I see how desperately and totally I need God's grace.

Beyond Self-Love and Self-Hate

While correcting our views of our own goodness and badness, the cross also moves us beyond those two characteristics into a beautiful personal freedom. The cross comprehends both our dignity and our depravity, but it centers on neither. Self is not forgotten, but neither is it dominant.

It is ironic to see how a dominant self often underlies even the "crucified life" teachings. For example, L. E. Maxwell cites Joseph, the son with the coat of many colors who was sold into slavery and suffered many injustices before he was exalted to govern all of Egypt. Maxwell writes, "God's way up for Joseph was down, as it must be for every disciple."

He then tells a touching story of a Civil War general named Howard, who permitted a rival to take his place of honor riding in review at the head of the corps because the commanding General Sherman said, "You are a Christian and can stand the disappointment." When Howard acquiesced, Sherman said, "Yes, let him have the honor, but you . . . will ride by my side at the head of the army."

Maxwell comments, "So it is with the saints who have humbled themselves under the mighty hand of God. The promise is that he will exalt you in due time."[4] My objection to all of this is that it is presented in the context of a plea for self-renunciation, for dying to self, for "putting the axe of the cross to the very root of the tree of self," as we quoted earlier. Now, it appears that what is aimed at all along is self-aggrandizement, getting to the top, being exalted. The "crucified believer" still wants to go up, and his going down is only a tactic to obtain the same self-serving ends others seek by more direct methods.

Please don't misunderstand. I am not saying that this desire to be exalted should be repugnant. Neither do I object to the idea that the proper path to such exaltation is the cross. Scripture often advances both of these ideas. What I object to is the rhetoric that suggests all self-seeking is wrong and then turns around and implicitly sanctions it. No wonder people get confused!

I have not intended anything in this chapter to be an attack on those with whom I disagree. Actually, I am persuaded that many people have been genuinely helped by the teachings of L. E. Maxwell. I am equally confident that many have been helped by the ministry of Robert Schuller.

I would guess that some have also been hindered by each man and the schools of thought they represent.

But who among us does all things well? Only Jesus.

And where on earth can we see truth revealed in perfect balance?

Only at the cross of Christ.

Lord, keep us faithful to that cross, with or without a clarion call.

1. L.E. Maxwell, *Born Crucified* (Chicago: Moody Press, 1945), p.59.

2. Robert H. Schuller, *Self-Esteem: The New Reformation* (Waco, Tex.: Word Books, 1982), p. 14.

3. Eugenia Price, *Leave Yourself Alone* (Grand Rapids, Mich: Zondervan, 1982).

4. Maxwell, pp. 179-80.

CHAPTER

9

WHAT?
ME DEAD
TO SIN?

I'm having trouble writing this book because of my sin. Here I am, writing about the cross, the central and most sacred reality in Christianity, and I'm doing it not only with severe human limitations but with unclean hands.

I don't mean that I'm aware of some specific controversy between me and God in which I'm rebelling and going my own way. That is not the case. I am acutely aware, however, that my life at its best comes far short of measuring up to the holiness of God.

> ... if even the heavens are not pure in his eyes,
> how much less man, who is vile and corrupt, who
> drinks up evil like water! (Job 15:15-16).

Even though I do not lap up iniquity as some do (or even as I once did), I'm still very far from being in God's class when it comes to holiness—so far, in fact, that it seems almost sacrilegious to mention my "holiness" and his in the same breath.

Much of the Bible serves to display in bold relief my deficiency in holiness. In ancient Israel, there was a Holy of Holies where God dwelt. No ordinary person—not even the priests—could enter that place, under pain of death. Only the High Priest could enter, and he but once a year, taking with him the appropriate sacrifice for his own sin and for the sins of the people. He wore bells on the hem of his garment so that those outside could hear the tinkle as he moved about performing his priestly duties. That way, they would know if he offended God's holiness and was struck dead (see Exodus 28:33-35).

I recall reading also about the Ark of the Covenant, a sacred piece of furniture from the Holy of Holies. A poor fellow named Uzzah was once helping to transport the Ark on a cart pulled by oxen. The oxen stumbled, Uzzah reached out to steady the Ark, and God struck him dead for touching it (1 Chronicles 13:7-10).

Who am I, then, that I presume to enter this Holiest place—the place of the cross, where God surely dwells? How can I dare to handle such sacred things?

I would give up the project—indeed would never have undertaken it in the first place—except for two considerations:

First, avoiding this task would not get me out of the Holy Place. Though I am keenly aware of the sacredness of the cross, the fact is that all of life is a Holy Place where God dwells. The Scripture says that my very body is the temple of God. I could decline the task of writing about the cross, but there is no way I can get away from the immediate presence of the Holy One, for he indwells me.

Second, God has given me a talent and told me to use it in his service. If I bury my talent, he will judge me a wicked and lazy servant. I am a steward not only of my writing ability but of whatever sacred truth I comprehend.

Paul said, "Woe to me if I do not preach the gospel!" (1 Corinthians 9:16). He viewed the message as a sacred trust which he had to communicate to others. He told the Romans that he was a debtor to all men to share a glorious gospel of which he was not ashamed. Sometimes Paul was ashamed of himself because he was a weak, earthen vessel. But he was not ashamed of the gospel because it is the power of God to salvation to everyone who believes. Paul could not let the shame of his own deficiencies keep him from proclaiming God's truth.

Neither can I. But what about my sin?

Two Bad Attitudes toward Sin

Our attitudes toward sin can and often do go astray in two opposite directions. We can be too careless or too careful, indifferent or overwrought, flippant or devastated, demonstrating no conscience or practically enduring the pangs of the damned.

We see these errors in well-known Bible characters. It's interesting, too, that while some may characteristically tend toward one extreme or the other, we can often observe both errors in the same person. How easy it is to err on one side or the other!

Take David for example. You would think the man had no conscience. He planned the murder of Uriah just to get him out of the way. It is hard to think of that as anything but the act of a person whose conscience was seared as with a hot iron, past feeling.

David's adultery with Bathsheba was bad enough, but it wasn't necessarily unconscionable. She was a beautiful woman; he was a lusty man; the circumstances lent themselves to an illicit alliance. David no doubt acted without malice.

Uriah's murder was altogether different. David planned it. He decided Uriah had to die even though he was innocent. At about the same time as this sorry incident took place, David was also perhaps involved in

-committing atrocities in war
-torturing prisoners
-seeking personal, unearned glory
-generally behaving abominably

The account in 2 Samuel 11 and 12 is subject to varying interpretations, but the picture of David is ugly at best. Certainly David's winking at sin during that time was contemptible.

This same man, however, showed an acutely tender conscience at other times. He apparently suffered pangs of guilt over the comparatively trivial offense of cutting off King Saul's coattail at a time when his companions thought he should have cut off Saul's head (see 1 Samuel 24:1-13).

At this point, things start getting sticky. Can we really say that an "acutely tender conscience" is a second "bad attitude" toward sin?

I think so, though I don't think David is a strong example of such a bad attitude. He understood grace too well to allow himself to wallow in self-reproach very long because of his sin.

So did Paul. He, like David, showed both insensitivity to sin (when he was killing Christians and hardening his heart against the Holy Spirit) and an acutely tender conscience (when he detected covetousness in his heart and called himself a wretched man because of it).

Covetousness! I heard one Catholic priest say that covetousness is the only commandment of the ten that he never hears about in the confessional. Among Protestants too, a covetous Christian, far from being called wretched, is likely to be passed off as an example of the man God blesses.

In any case, Paul was like David in that he understood grace too well to be a strong example of a bad attitude toward sin.

But then there was Judas—callousness personified. He could sell out Jesus to his enemies for thirty pieces of silver and from there go brazenly to the Lord's table to fellowship with the other apostles. When Jesus announced that one of them would betray him, Judas could say with a straight face, "Surely not I, Rabbi?" (Matthew 26:25).

Yet this same man was so overcome with remorse a little later that he threw the blood money down in the temple and went out and hanged himself. He was dead even before Jesus was.

Now, that is a bad attitude toward sin.

Two Bad Results

In Judas, especially, and to a lesser degree in David and Paul, we see not only extreme indifference toward sin and extreme sensitivity to it, but we also see the bad results of both. Indifference toward sin makes us destroy other people while extreme sensitivity makes us self-destructive. Insensitivity to sin made Paul and David men of violence and blood, and it made Judas a traitor. Extreme sensitivity made Paul and David miserable, and it made Judas a suicide.

The consequences of extreme sensitivity were worse with Judas because he did not know God's grace. David and Paul did.

David described his inner anguish over sin in Psalm 51. "For I know my transgression and my sin is always before me. Against you, you only, have I sinned and done what is evil in your sight, so that you are proved right when you speak and justified when you judge" (vv. 3-4).

The heart-cry of the sin-sensitive soul is, "Whatever happens to me, I deserve it and worse."

This nether land of misery and woe is hardly where God wants us to take up residence. David passed through such a "slough of despond," but he didn't settle down there. As we have said, David knew and always kept in mind that the grace of God was greater than his sin. In celebration of that grace in his own life he wrote: "Blessed is he whose transgressions are forgiven, whose sins are covered. Blessed is the man whose sin the LORD does not count against him and in whose spirit is no deceit" (Psalm 32:1-2).

Paul understood grace, too. His "What a wretched man I am!" of Romans 7 is sandwiched between "Our old self was crucified with him that the body of sin might be rendered powerless, that we should no longer be slaves to sin" (Romans 6:6), and "Therefore, there is now no condemnation for those who are in Christ Jesus" (Romans 8:1). The earlier passage points the way to victory, and the latter one expresses assurance of forgiveness. These are the solutions to sin, offering both prevention and remedy.

Oh, to Grace, How Great a Stranger!

We live in the "age of grace." God deals with us not according to our sin but according to his great love and mercy. We hear that, maybe even preach it, but we often fall far short of realizing it to the extent that David and Paul did, though David supposedly lived "under the law."

When our tender consciences condemn us, our attitude toward sin often becomes bad. We see ourselves as unfit for God, rash intruders into the Holy Place.

Joseph R. Cooke was one who long entertained this bad attitude. It didn't result in his suicide, but it came close. Though he was trained in theology and preached the grace of God, his sense of sinfulness led to a nervous breakdown. He left his mission work in Thailand, unable any longer to teach, preach, or even read his Bible.

Cooke describes the attitude that led to his breakdown:

> God's demands of me were so high, and his opinion of me so low, there was no way for me to live except under his frown . . . . All day long he nagged me: "Why don't you pray more? Why don't you witness more? When will you ever learn self-discipline? How can you allow yourself to indulge in such wicked thoughts? Do this. Don't do that. Yield, confess, work harder. . . ." God was always using his love against me. He'd show me his nail-pierced hands, and then he would look at me glaringly and say, "Well, why aren't you a better Christian? Get busy and live the way you ought to."
>
> Most of all, I had a God who down underneath considered me to be less than dirt. Oh, he made a great ado about loving me, but I believed that the day-to-day love and acceptance I longed for could only be mine if I let him crush nearly everything that was really me. When I came down to it, there was scarcely a word or a feeling or a thought or a decision of mine that God really liked.[1]

What a Mess!

What are we to do? If we give ourselves any rein, we are likely to fall into desperate sin like David did. We must take sin deadly seriously. But if we take it so seriously and elevate our standards to a level anywhere near God's holiness, how will we live with ourselves? How can we function? How can we abide in the Holy Place when we are so unholy?

One way out is to soften our definition of sin. That is what many do. For example, in the classic book *Sin and*

Temptation by John Owen, first published in the mid-17th century, we read:

> 1. The will is the cause of obedience or disobedience. Moral actions are willed. An ancient sage said: "Every sin is so voluntary, that if it is not voluntary, it is not sin." The will actualizes sin or obedience.

> 2. The will consents to sin. The will does this in two ways. Sometimes, after full and complete deliberation, the will becomes wholly convinced, weakened, or conquered. With this general, overall consent, the will goes to sea like a ship in full sail. Or it rushes into sin like a horse into battle. People do this, says the apostle, "giving themselves over to sin with greediness" (Ephesians 4:19). Ahab, for example, deliberately murdered Naboth (1 Kings 21).

> On the other hand, someone's will to sin may come in conflict with his other desires. Peter's will to deny his Master conflicted with his love for Christ. If he had not willed to deny him, he would not have done so. Even then, he did not deny Christ with pleasure, but rather with grief and repentance (Matthew 26:75).[2]

Again, we read on the next page of the same book: "Where there is no will, as we have seen, there is no sin."

Such a teaching could serve to relieve the mind of an over-sensitive person. He or she might think, "Since I did not will to do wrong, I have not really sinned."

This teaching, however, will not stand scrutiny. Scripture teaches that wrongdoing is sin whether we choose, will, or intend wrong or not. In fact, our wrongdoing is still sin when, far from willing it, we don't even know we did wrong. Leviticus 4 and 5 deals with many such situations. One verse sums up much of the teaching: "If a person sins and does what is forbidden in any of the Lord's commands, even though he does not know it, he is guilty and will be held responsible" (5:17). The sixteenth verse speaks of making restitution "for what he has failed to do," suggesting that sins of omission are also sins whether intended or not.

With this, the New Testament implicitly agrees. For example, when Paul, before his conversion, was persecuting Christians, he undoubtedly thought he was doing God a service. He was not willfully sinning. He later wrote, "Even though I was once a blasphemer and a persecutor and a violent man, I was shown mercy because I acted in ignorance and unbelief" (1 Timothy 1:13). His ignorance may have been grounds for showing him mercy, but it did not excuse him from needing mercy. It didn't keep his wrongdoing from being sin. Indeed, Paul wrote only a few lines later, "Christ Jesus came into the world to save sinners—of whom I am the worst" (v. 15).

The Way Out

In the Leviticus passage cited above, God's people were told repeatedly that they must bring the prescribed offerings even for unintentional sins. Christ is our offering, the Lamb of God who died on the cross for all our sins. We continually need the covering he provided there. Thank God, we also may continually claim that covering!

That's why there is no condemnation to those who are in Christ Jesus. Not because we can juggle the rules downward and our behavior upward to the point where we pass muster. No, we don't pass muster. We are guilty. There is no reprieve, no excuse, no getting out of it. We deserve to die.

The good news is that in Christ, we did die. Now we are "dead to sin" in the sense that no claims or charges remain unsatisfied against us. We can get on with our lives. God is not frowning!

Dead to Sin Also Means Don't Live In Sin

The cross is the answer to an acute over-sensitivity to sin. It also corrects that other bad attitude—presumption, the idea that we can go ahead and sin because everybody does it and it's all covered by grace anyhow.

The cross cuts right through our inconsistent attitudes toward sin and calls us to live on another plane.

WHAT? ME DEAD TO SIN?

This is what we read:

> We died to sin; how can we live in it any longer?
> Or don't you know that all of us who were bap-
> tized into Christ Jesus were baptized into his
> death? . . . The death he died, he died to sin once
> for all; but the life he lives, he lives to God. In the
> same way, count yourselves dead to sin but alive
> to God in Jesus Christ. Therefore, do not let sin
> reign in your mortal body (Romans 6:2-3,10-12).

The basic principle set forth here is that we who believe in Christ are united with him. We were "baptized into Christ Jesus."

Forget about water and ritual for a moment, because that's not what the passage is talking about. When we receive Christ as Savior, a spiritual transaction takes place. We are "baptized by one Spirit into one body" (1 Corinthians 12:13). We become spiritually united with Christ and with all other Christians. When this happens, water baptism is an appropriate outward expression of the inward spiritual reality.

But the central truth we must grasp is that we are never again going to be alienated or cut off from the life of God. We have a real spiritual union with Christ. We have become God's children by being born spiritually into his family. We are now partakers of the divine nature (see 2 Peter 1:4).

Previously we had only an Adamic nature, to which sin comes inescapably and naturally—or so it seems. But now we have a new lineage. We are a different breed of cat, so to speak. We are Christ-ones.

Based on this union with Christ, we are to count or reckon ourselves dead to sin by virtue of the crucifixion and alive to God by virtue of the resurrection.

Many Christians have difficulty with this reckoning. They read Scripture. They hear teaching. They encounter the "dead to sin" message and try to do or not do or trust or mortify or resist or be filled or "let go and let God" or die. Still they sin. To say that they are dead to sin seems like shameless posturing, like hypocrisy. They are dead to sin about as much as ducks hate water and alcoholics loathe booze.

As a result, even the passage that is supposed to help them causes consternation. Maybe I'm not really born again, they think. How come I'm so far from being dead to sin?

It's clear from the language of the passage, however, that "dead to sin" is not to be understood as an incapacity to respond to sin. If that were the case, no reckoning or counting would be necessary—or possible. Sin would simply no longer be an issue.

Will the Real You Please Stand?

"Count yourselves dead to sin and alive to God" means that you should view sin as something alien to your true nature. Despite what we've said about God's holiness being far above ours even at our best, it's also true that sin is not native to the human species. Adam and Eve were not created as sinners. Sin entered from without. Jesus Christ came upon the scene as one fully human (as well as divine); yet he lived and died without sin.

Even as a human being, then, you are not intrinsically sinful. Sin is an intruder, a cancer of the soul, an outside influence that has taken control.

As a Christian, you are even less an intrinsic host to sin than you were as a child of Adam. You have been born again into the family of God. God's seed in you is holy and cannot sin. You are on your way to an eternal kingdom where "nothing impure will ever enter" (Revelation 21:27). You are going to feel at home there. Totally at home, as you have never been before. You will not long for the old ways or the old days. You will not secretly miss your sins, for you will fully know that they were never really a part of you. They do not belong.

It is to this that Paul alludes in Romans 7. Speaking of the sins that still troubled his life, he said, "It is no longer I who do it, but it is sin living in me that does it" (v. 20).

This is no attempt to evade responsibility. Paul is not saying, "It's OK if I sin because it's not really me doing it."

But he does say that "it is no longer I." Sinful behavior does not represent who and what he is—a child of God. It rather represents the malignant entity, sin, which is operative in his life.

From Evildoers Come Evil Deeds

The cross took care of the penalty for our sins because we died there in union with Christ. It also took care of the power of sin over us, and for the same reason.

Then why does sin still exert its power over us? For the same reason sin still exacts its penalty from sinners. Though the cross provided the payment for sin, the provision has to be claimed by faith. Those who do not claim it perish under the law.

The process of being saved from the power of sin involves claiming the provisions of the cross. It requires that we develop a new way of looking at reality.

The old way of looking at reality was to see myself as a slave to sin. The new way is to see myself as dead to sin and alive to God through the crucifixion and resurrection of Christ, the head of the new race to which I now belong.

Earlier we spoke of David's remarkable understanding of grace. He also said something that reveals the beautiful insight he and others of ancient times had into the concept of being God's righteous people, not "sinners."

It was on the occasion when David cut off Saul's coat-tail but spared his life. David explained why he would not harm Saul even though Saul was trying to kill him. He said he was not going to do evil just because others did. "My hand will not touch you," he assured Saul.

Then David said something we all need to take to heart. It was an "old saying" already in David's time: "From evildoers come evil deeds" (1 Samuel 24:13).

David didn't see himself as an evildoer, so it wasn't for him to do evil deeds. "In the same way, count yourselves dead to sin but alive to God in Christ Jesus. Therefore do not let sin reign in your mortal body so that you obey its evil desires. Do not offer the parts of your body to sin, as instruments of wickedness, but rather offer yourselves to

God, as those who have been brought from death to life; and offer the parts of your body to him as instruments of righteousness. For sin shall not be your master, because you are not under law, but under grace" (Romans 6:11-14).

But suddenly here comes sin. I fall.

What now?

I have a choice. I can accept this sin as *me*. If I do, my life will follow a predictable pattern. I will plunge into defeat. I may say, "What's the use? I've tried and tried and failed again and again." I may beat myself, try harder, weep more bitterly, promise more fervently. Eventually I may drive myself to suicide or a nervous breakdown. Or I may grow disillusioned with Christianity and wander off into the wilderness of a life out of fellowship with God.

But there is a second and better choice. I can refuse to identify myself with this sin. I can say, "This is *not me*. Sin is *in* me, tempting me, tripping me, taunting me. But I am crucified with Christ. I am dead to sin and alive to God. I know where I'm headed, and guess what? Sin is not coming along, for nothing impure will enter there."

So rage on, sin, for a little while; but you'll find less and less response from me. Your venomous strikes and your contortions are the death throes of a dying serpent. Long after you are no more, I will live forever with Christ.

1. Joseph R. Cooke, *Free for the Taking* (Old Tappan, N.J.: Revell, 1975), quoted in David Seamands, *Healing for Damaged Emotions* (Wheaton, Ill.: Victor, 1981), p. 84

2. John Owen, *Sin and Temptation* (Portland, OR: Multnomah Press, 1983), p. 65.

PART FIVE

Where the Cross Leads

10

EVER-INCREASING GLORY

Some time ago I went to my brother's house and was invited to inspect his latest project, a built-in kitchen table and some wine racks. Being in sales all of his adult life, Ron had never before done much with his hands. Now, rather pleased with his efforts, he wanted to show me the results of his handiwork.

Ron had done a commendable job. The work was not that of a professional—he could have bought something nicer, and for less money, too, if one considers the value of the time invested. But struggling with wood and tools to fashion a work of value gave Ron a deep satisfaction that would have been lacking had he simply purchased the items or hired someone to do the work.

The Price of Glory

Satisfaction, joy, glory within—these deepest treasures of the human spirit cannot be bought. Neither can they be gratuitously bestowed upon us by another. Glory—even of the earthly variety—has a personal price attached to it, and that price, in turn, has a cross-like quality about it.

In our society, for example, sports figures get a lot of glory. But we who look on, cheering and perhaps envying, little know how hard our athlete heroes worked and how much they endured before they captured any glory.

Take divers. Almost anyone able to swim can throw himself or herself into a pool of water and emerge "successfully." But one does not get into the Olympics that way. You have to go off the high board, execute precise flips and turns, and enter the water with skill and grace.

That's not easy! I've been off the high board many times, but nobody ever urged me to try for the Olympics. I guess no one was impressed with my straight-down, feet-first, hold-your-nose style. I did try diving head-first once. I wrenched my neck and stung my forehead when I smacked into the water, and that was that. A *guy could get hurt this way*, I thought, correctly.

While I derived some enjoyment out of leaping into the pool feet first, I never got any glory out of it. Diving glory involves something they call "degree of difficulty." In Olympic competition, the more difficult a dive, the more points it's worth. The medals go to the divers who best execute the most difficult dives.

In rodeo it's the same. You don't win the silver buckle for staying astride some old nag that hardly bucks. Riding a bronc that turns and twists worse than a rowboat at sea in a hurricane is what racks up the points.

And they don't give a football team the Superbowl trophy for beating any eleven guys from out back in the stock room. You have to beat the best professional players in the country.

It's the same in all walks of life: business, industry, the professions—even our hobbies like Ron's woodworking. There is a cross-like shadow over achievement in any field. Costly devotion and self-sacrifice must precede glory.

Glory or Vainglory

While everything worthwhile costs, not everything that costs is worthwhile. We can knock ourselves out seeking glory and only hurt ourselves and others in the process. Hitler comes quickly to mind. He was ready to sacrifice anything and everything in pursuit of his glorious dream of a "thousand-year Reich." It was not lack of dedication or purpose that covered his name with lasting shame rather than glory.

Paying a cross-like price is necessary to gaining glory, but it isn't enough. We also need a cross-like commitment to the will of God. We need that proper focus on God's will in preference to our own (of which we wrote in the first chapter of this book).

Otherwise our pursuit of glory becomes vainglory, even though it may clothe itself in the garb of Christian life and service.

John Claypool, a Baptist preacher, is a good example of one whose driving pursuit of glory was really vainglory. He writes:

> People used to ask me what I wanted to be when I grew up, and I was shrewd enough to fashion my answer according to what I thought they wanted to hear. For some it was a policeman, for others a fireman or preacher. However, in my own heart of hearts, I had my own private fantasy that I never dared to share with anyone. Do you know what it was? I am telling you the gospel truth: *I wanted to be president of the world*!
>
> I envisioned the whole human race as a giant triangle with one place of preeminence at the top. I dreamed of climbing over everybody's back until at last I got there. Then I knew exactly what I would do. I would look down and say, "Now! Now, do I amount to something? Have I at last become a somebody out of my nobodiness?"[1]

Claypool saw himself as competing for glory with the rest of the human race. There was "one place of preeminence at the top." If he didn't get there, he lost out on the glory of being somebody. When Claypool was converted to Christ, and even when he entered the ministry, this basic approach to life was unchanged:

> I must say, also, that life in the parish ministry has not been a whole lot different. I can still recall going to state and national conventions in our denomination and coming home feeling drained and unclean, because most of the conversation in the hotel rooms and the halls was characterized either by envy of those who were doing well or scarcely concealed delight for

those who were doing poorly. For did not that mean that someone was about to fall, and would thus create an opening higher up the ladder?

This grasping for personal glory took its toll and led to a personal crisis for Claypool:

> About ten years out of seminary I began to feel a variety of disquieting emotions. For one thing, I was really bone-weary. Do you have any idea how much energy it takes always to have to succeed and come out number one? I was also beginning to sense how lonely and isolated this way of living leaves one. How can you really relate openly and warmly to persons when you realize that at a deeper level you are competing with them and trying to outdo them?[2]

The glory of the cross has nothing to do with a destructive and competitive drive to prove we are somebody. The glory of the cross belongs to those who, like Christ, already know they are somebody but are willing to set aside personal rights and desires in order to do the will of God.

Performing at 130 Percent

While everything worthwhile costs, we aren't asked to give more than we have. Glory from athletic exploits such as the high dive is for those who can perform flawlessly, but the glory of the cross is for ordinary people.

Only Christ is perfect; we are not. His cross sufficed to redeem a fallen world. We have to settle for far less. Nothing we can do will save the world. Our glory may lie in simply being "useful" to the work of God.

J. B. Phillips was one who found it difficult to settle for the limited glory of being merely useful. Phillips gained worldwide fame as an author and as translator of the Scriptures. Yet he suffered immensely much of his life from a sense of not having achieved enough. Early in his ministry, he made personal notes about his feelings of inadequacy, an inner need to perform at "130 percent," as he called it. He jotted down, "Rather die than be ordinary." And again he noted, "No praise, no admiration—just usefulness— how I hate just to be useful."[3]

In later years Phillips endured much personal anguish of soul and mind, and counseled others who were also suffering. One woman wrote that she had served God actively but was now paralyzed and lacked a sense of purpose. She wrote: "Was the idea that my hands, feet, voice, intellect were being used by God just a piece of arrogant, self-glorifying imagination? It certainly seems so now."

Phillips implored her not to "think that all we knew and felt, and almost saw, in happier days was only illusion. Of course, it was no such thing. Do you imagine that Christ himself was not in an agony of doubt both in Gethsemane and on the cross? How cruelly he must have been tempted to believe that all that he had previously thought and proclaimed was no more than self-delusion."

He also told her, "But one of the things I am sure is true is that we must not (as C. S. Lewis once wrote) 'lament over past raptures.' If we can look back and be thankful that we were useful, active and self-giving, fine. But to look back and feel nothing but misery that we can no longer do what we once did is surely soul-destroying."[4]

Note that Phillips once agonized over being "just useful," but he later saw being useful as a glorious treasure. Still, it was easier for him to counsel others than to heed his own wise words.

These, then, are great evils, to seek glory by excelling over others (as Claypool did) or to seek to perform perfectly. But they are not the only errors one can make. Before we cast stones at those on ego trips and out to build kingdoms for themselves, let us examine whether we have a beam in our own eye.

No Glory in Mediocrity

For every person like J.B. Phillips, who had to perform at 130 percent, or like John Claypool, who wanted to be president of the world, there must be a dozen who have no significant goals or dreams. Some gave up their dreams years ago or they never had any. Others cherish trivial hopes and dreams that would be essentially meaningless even if they were fulfilled.

One winner of a state lottery was asked what he intended to do with his money. "The first thing I'll do is buy a new pickup," he said; "that has been my lifetime goal."

There's nothing wrong with wanting and buying a new pickup. But to have that as one's lifetime goal?

It's hard to know just why we sometimes languish without dreams or settle for unworthy goals. Perhaps we have given in to laziness, defeat, ridicule, or opposition. Perhaps we have an ego problem opposite to Claypool's. He felt he wasn't really somebody unless he was top dog. Maybe we feel uneasy about pursuing a dream, or even having one because that includes an element of seeking great things for ourselves. We sometimes imagine that wanting glory is not a Christian or spiritual desire.

C. S. Lewis, for one, declared such an attitude to be misguided:

> If there lurks in most modern minds the notion that to desire our own good and earnestly to hope for the enjoyment of it is a bad thing, I submit that this notion has crept in from Kant and the Stoics and is no part of the Christian faith. Indeed, if we consider the unblushing promises of reward and the staggering nature of the rewards promised in the Gospels, it would seem that our Lord finds our desires, not too strong, but too weak. We are half-hearted creatures, fooling about with drink and sex and ambition when infinite joy is offered us, like an ignorant child who wants to go on making mud pies in a slum because he cannot imagine what is meant by the offer of a holiday at the sea. . . . We are far too easily pleased.[5]

What I am calling glory, Lewis calls "infinite joy." It is to be contrasted with crass ambition; it's not the same thing. It isn't being president of the world or outperforming everybody else; neither is it being content merely to live out one's life with a full belly and a color TV.

Where Is the Glory?

Jesus was the one man who truly deserved to be king of the world when he walked upon this earth, but his only crown was made of thorns. Not only was his dream denied, it was mocked. Unfeeling soldiers dressed him in a robe of royal purple, put a stick in his hand and called it a scepter, then knelt before him and taunted him with "Hail, King of the Jews!" (see Matthew 27:27-30).

When Jesus was approaching this cosmic travesty, he uttered some striking words in prayer, words that give us important clues to finding glory whatever our personal circumstances may be. It is not Jesus' prayer in the Garden to which we look now, but another pre-crucifixion prayer.

The scene was the upper room. The Lord's Supper had been instituted, Jesus had washed the disciples' feet, Judas had gone out to betray the Lord, and the agony of the Garden and the crucifixion were only hours away.

Jesus began to pray:

> Father, the time has come. Glorify your Son, that your Son may glorify you. . . . I have brought you glory on earth by completing the work you gave me to do. And now, Father, glorify me in your presence with the glory I had with you before the world began (John 17:1-5).

Strongly dominating not only this part but all of the prayer is the theme of *glory*. This seems a strange theme to associate with the shameful and humiliating death of the cross, an experience that Jesus was presently to beg the Father to spare him.

How could Jesus refer to the cross as his glorification?

Look at it this way. Christ's whole purpose and destiny was to glorify God. Glorifying God brought him his highest fulfillment. Since it was at the cross that Jesus glorified God supremely, the cross also fulfilled his own joy and destiny more than anything else.

That's where the glory is for us as well. We were made to glorify God. We were redeemed to glorify God. Like Jesus did, we have to take up the cross in order to glorify God; that's when the glory comes.

In chapter two we examined what it means to be blessed. Mary the mother of Jesus was blessed above all other women. Not that she had more pleasant circumstances. She did not. Ultimately a sword pierced her soul. But she was blessed in that she knew a great sense of meaning and purpose as mother of Messiah.

If having a sense of purpose is a blessing, then to experience the fulfillment of that purpose is truly glorious.

Notice that theme in Jesus' prayer, cited above: "I have brought you glory on earth *by completing the work you gave me to do. And now, Father, glorify me . . .*"

Every time we complete a work God gives us to do, there is glory. And when we complete our entire life's work, we can echo the glorious shout of the apostle Paul at the end of his life:

"I have fought the good fight.
"I have finished the race.
"I have kept the faith.
"Now there is in store for me the crown . . . "
(2 Timothy 4:7-8)

Glory or Glitter?

Sometimes what we lose in taking up the cross to do the will of God may in itself seem glorious. Satan offered Jesus "all the kingdoms of this world and their splendor" if Jesus would bow down and worship Satan. Jesus chose the way of the cross instead, for it led to true and lasting glory. Satan's offer, based on rebellion against God, was bound to lead to disaster.

Moses, too, gave up a "glorious" kingdom for the greater glory of the cross. We read it in Hebrews 11:24-26:

By faith Moses, when he had grown up, refused to be known as the son of Pharaoh's daughter. He chose to be mistreated along with the people of God rather than to enjoy the pleasures of sin for a short time. He regarded disgrace for the sake of Christ as of greater value than the treasures of Egypt, because he was looking ahead to his reward.

What insight this passage gives us into Moses' thought processes. Exodus tells us the facts as they happened, but here we see into Moses' heart.

When Moses turned his back on all that it meant to be a prince in the household of Pharaoh, he gave up more than most of us could ever hope to gain. The before and after picture of Moses' life was not one most of us would covet.

BEFORE	AFTER
Fame as a prince of Egypt	Shame as a Hebrew slave
Material wealth, splendor	Poverty, mere subsistence
Privilege and power	Cultural deprivation
Power	Outsider status

In many ways Moses paralleled the Lord Jesus Christ, who would later make virtually the same sacrifices (although infinitely greater!) in leaving heaven for earth and its cross!

Yet Moses did all this because "he regarded disgrace for the sake of Christ as of greater value than the treasures of Egypt." This wasn't a minus for Moses. He wasn't losing out. He gave up much in order to gain infinitely more. He gave up the glitter of Egypt for the glory of the cross.

Just so, taking up the cross is not something we do with a sense of self-sacrifice or loss, even though we do it with eyes wide open as to the cost. The glory we gain is worth far more than anything we lose.

Glory Now and Later

It's not uncommon to hear that "a cross now leads to a crown hereafter." We used to sing it:

If you don't bear the cross,
then you can't wear the crown,
'way beyond the blue.

That is a biblical concept. It was true even for Jesus, as we read in Philippians 2:

And being found in appearance as a man, he humbled himself and became obedient unto death—even death on a cross! Therefore God

exalted him to the highest place and gave him
the name that is above every name, that at the
name of Jesus every knee should bow, in heaven
and on earth and under the earth, and every
tongue confess that Jesus Christ is Lord, to the
glory of God the Father" (vv. 8-11).

It was because Jesus humbled himself to the death of
the cross that God exalted him. Though he had glory before
he ever came to earth, and glory while he was on the earth,
he has greater glory with the redeemed multitudes loving
and worshiping him forever.

This greater glory was not something Jesus had at the
time of the crucifixion. He doesn't fully possess it even yet,
since every knee has not yet bowed to him nor has every
tongue confessed him Lord.

Yet Jesus said just before his death, "Now is the Son of
man glorified" (John 13:31). He said, "The time has come"
to be glorified (John 17:1). He could have been speaking in
anticipation of the coming exaltation and glory; but why
should we assume that? Perhaps he meant just what he
said. Anticipating the future glory did not eclipse the glory
of that hour for Jesus.

There is without a doubt a future glory awaiting us, too,
as we follow Christ. Paul wrote that "our present sufferings
are not worth comparing with the glory that will be revealed in us" (Romans 8:18). But there is also a glory now,
and like Jesus we ought to seize upon the now glory while
we are waiting for the future.

Once we understand this we can, Moses-like, take up
our cross with joy. It's true that there is a price to pay. We
should not, and in this book we certainly have not,
minimized the suffering involved in the cross. God suffered, Christ suffered, Mary suffered, the apostles suffered,
we will suffer.

That doesn't mean, however, that we should be doleful
about bearing the cross—reluctant, as if we begrudge making so great a sacrifice. Those who truly bear the cross do
not congratulate themselves on what exceptionally good
Christians they have been, how much faith they have, or

what sterling examples of spiritual devotion they are. As long as any of this false martyr spirit characterizes us, we have not yet understood the glory of the cross.

Ever-Increasing Glory

Scripture says there is an "ever-increasing glory" that can be ours. In saying this, Paul recalls the man who chose glory over glitter—Moses. Paul writes that "the Israelites could not look steadily at the face of Moses because of its glory, fading though it was" (2 Corinthians 3:7). Paul alludes to the shining face Moses had when he came down from Mt. Sinai after receiving the Ten Commandments the second time from God.

That glory in the face of Moses faded. By contrast, Paul writes, "we . . . are being transformed into his likeness with ever-increasing glory, which comes from the Lord, who is the Spirit" (v. 18).

Most glory fades. Glory is hard to come by and even harder to keep. Not many boys or girls grow up to be president of the United States. Even those who make it to the White House have to step down sometime, usually to spend the rest of their lives in relative obscurity.

Not many Christians become household names. Those few who do reach the pinnacle of success have difficulty staying there. Most either fade or fall.

It's the same in all walks of life: business, industry, entertainment, the professions.

Even the limited glory of fulfilling modest lifetime dreams is often elusive. A few years ago I wrote the life story of Faye and Bill Pruitt. While growing up in a preacher's home, Faye's goal was to marry a good Christian man and have a godly family. Such a desire seems wholly appropriate and realistic.

But the path to Faye's humble goal was strewn with pitfalls. She became engaged to the wrong man and almost married him, extricating herself from the relationship only with great difficulty. Then she fell in love with Bill Pruitt, but within one week after their engagement she suffered injuries in an auto accident that left her paralyzed below the waist.

Overcoming the odds, she and Bill did marry and they had children. But their marriage encountered severe strains, and Faye's original dream seemed all but lost. Even my part in the modified dream—writing a book to redeem some of the suffering by telling the story to God's glory—met with frustration. We couldn't find a publisher. Some said the book was too much like *Joni*.

So Faye is redundant? The world doesn't need her?

Or is there some way to impart glory to life even when our hopes and dreams turn to ashes?

Paul says there is a lasting and ever-growing glory which comes from the Lord. It's a glory that starts ingloriously, at the cross.

I think Proverbs describes it well: "The path of the righteous is like the first gleam of dawn, shining ever brighter till the full light of day" (4:18). At the cross there was darkness over the whole earth, and the cross still seems a dark experience for us. But it is at the cross our light first truly begins to dawn. And that light will go on shining, brighter and brighter, clear into eternity.

The same passage in Proverbs also describes the alternative: "But the way of the wicked is like deep darkness; they do not know what makes them stumble" (v. 19). We are right now in God's day that is growing ever brighter . . . or we are in a darkness that will only deepen into eternal night.

As stated earlier, the greatest and most glorious thing any of us can ever do is to glorify God by obeying his will. We might get all excited if we were being considered for president of the United States (or of the world!). The man with the shining face chose to give up that kind of "glory" for something better—to cast his lot with a slave class because that was God's call.

Some of us would think it the ultimate if we were on top of the heap as Christian celebrities. We feel discouraged because we are not what we had hoped, and our disappointment is all the keener because we wanted to glorify God in some big way, yet we haven't done so.

But glorifying God isn't a matter of making a big splash. Glorifying God doesn't require earthly status, money, or talent. What it does require is that we know to whom we belong.

"Do you not know that your body is a temple of the Holy Spirit, who is in you, whom you have received from God? You are not your own;" (1 Corinthians 6:19 KJV). It is not *who* we are that counts so much as *whose* we are. We must settle forever the question of whose we are and whom we serve.

A Daily Glory

Beyond settling the question of whose I am, I can also glorify God by what I do. We read in Scripture such down-to-earth admonitions as, "So whether you eat or drink or whatever you do, do it all for the glory of God" (1 Corinthians 10:31).

How does one eat or drink to the glory of God? In many ways. One way is by giving thanks to God for the provision. A second is by maintaining wholesome eating and drinking practices that enhance the health of our bodies, which are his temples. A third is by avoiding those indulgences which might offend another's faith. A fourth is by enjoying our food and drink in Christ-honoring fellowship with others, extending hospitality to the people of God. A fifth is by remembering the poor when we eat and providing something to them in Jesus' name.

We further read: "you were bought at a price. Therefore, honor God with your body" (1 Corinthians 6:20).

Here we are told that we don't have to be king of the world to glorify God, but we do need to be king over our bodies. It is a glory to us when we glorify God in our bodies. Again, we can do that in many ways. One is to keep them pure from sexual sin. A second is to keep them healthy and in shape. A third is to keep them well-groomed and attractive. A fourth is to keep their members active in serving God: using the tongue to praise him, the eyes to read his Word, the ears to hear the cries of the oppressed, the hands to serve human need, the feet to take us on our Master's business, the mind to search out his truth.

Many of the things we must do to glorify God involve self-denial. They require us to take up our cross. Doing so will mean glory hereafter. It also means glory now—the unsurpassed glory of knowing we have done the will of God. We have fulfilled our function on earth. We have done what we were created to do.

Every moment lived to the glory of God is a moment of glory for us. No one can take it away. No former or future delinquencies can cancel it out. This moment we were obedient to the divine purpose. This moment we were once and forever what we were made to be. This moment is *ours*!

Multiplying the Glory

If a moment lived to the glory of God is a moment of glory for us in the fulfillment of our destinies, what we need to do is multiply such moments. At this point, our dreams of glory can become a stumbling block if we so want to be president of the world that we muff our chances to be president of our lives; if we want so much to be what we cannot be that we fail to be what we are to the glory of God.

The story goes that in seventeenth-century Italy there lived a young man named Antonio, who dearly loved good music. His soul thrilled to hear the great performers and composers of his day. How he yearned to glorify God with such enraptured music! But try as he would, he could neither compose nor perform with anything better than mediocre results. It became clear to Antonio that he would never be a great musician.

What bitter irony! Why would God give him a soul for music but no talent to match? All he could do was work with his hands.

Antonio mourned his dashed dreams for a time, but at last decided that if he could not play fine instruments, he would make them. He began to fashion violins with utmost care and devotion. From these instruments, he decided, must come forth the beautiful melodies he had in his soul but could not produce.

Today the grand voices and talented performers of Antonio's time have long since been silenced by the grave. But wherever great music at its best is played and loved, the violins of Antonio Stradivarius still sing the melodies of his heart.

You can bring glory to God. It doesn't matter who you are. It doesn't matter what your talents are. It doesn't matter whether you are known or unknown, understood or misunderstood, appreciated or despised.

Do not give up the dream. Why should you mark time waiting for death to make official the futility of a life that has long since ended?

But how can things be different? What can you do to experience the glory?

The Answer Is in the Cross

Jesus said, "Anyone who does not take his cross and follow me is not worthy of me. Whoever finds his life will lose it and whoever loses his life for my sake will find it" (Matthew 10:38-39).

Strange, isn't it, how people cling to their own little lives long after they have turned sour? They no longer have anything worth saving. Yet they follow a pattern long established in their lives—a pattern of self-seeking, self-saving, self-serving.

Jesus offers something so much better. He offers a cross—an opportunity to save your life by losing it.

It will mean getting your life into proper focus, centering on God's will rather than your own wishes. Even your strongest desires will be offered up before God as you pray, like Jesus, "Yet not as I will but as You will" (Matthew 26:39).

Taking up your cross will also mean reappraising what you think constitutes God's blessing on your life. Over and above all creature comforts, you will value the meaning and purpose that you find in being God's person doing God's will.

Living by cross purposes means you will distinguish between life's incidentals and its fundamentals. To have prosperity, health, and happy circumstances as traveling companions through life will be fine with you, but you will never allow them to take over the itinerary.

In taking up the cross you will consistently renounce the tactics of the flesh as a means of serving God. You will be more ready to suffer for Christ than to inflict suffering in his name. You will be more ready to love people into the Kingdom of God than to force them, knowing that "man's anger does not bring about the righteous life that God desires" (James 1:20). You will not abuse your power.

As a bearer of the cross, you will realize that at a deep level you have identified with the ultimate reality that is God. The Father, the Son, and the Holy Spirit compassionately interact with man's suffering. That is what the cross is—the compassionate suffering of deity along with and on behalf of his creatures. Incredible as it seems, when you take up the cross you become a partaker of the sufferings of Christ and a part of God's healing team.

The cross will also work some wonderful changes in you. It will free you from the detrimental extremes of self-love and self-hate as it demonstrates both your great need and your great worth in the eyes of God.

The cross will become God's wonderful solution to your sin problem. You will neither be crushed beneath the guilt of your sin nor will you shrug off sin as something to be taken lightly. In the cross, you died, so no further penalty is due you. Your guilt is gone and you are pronounced righteous. That same cross delivers you into a new life, not now as an evildoer but as a bonafide member of that eternal kingdom where "nothing impure will ever enter" (Revelation 21:27).

Finally, taking up the cross will invest your life with something ineffable. Words are inadequate to describe the quality of life to which the cross leads—that new life which Jesus said we find by losing the old one. We cannot describe it, but can only define it with one cryptic word—*glory*. It's a word we all know but none of us fully understands.

Jesus gave us a glimpse of the glory to which we move when he prayed for us just before his crucifixion. "Father, I want those you have given me to be with me where I am, and to see my glory, the glory you have given me because you loved me before the creation of the world" (John 17:24).

Think of it! To be with Jesus! To see his eternal glory! That would be something!

But Jesus wasn't through praying yet. He concluded by asking even more. "Righteous Father, . . . I have made you known to them and will continue to make you known in order that the love you have for me may be in them and that I myself may be in them" (vv. 25-26).

We are:

Progressively to know the Father better!

To be loved by the Father with the same love he has for Christ!

To have Christ in us!

That is glory, glory available to all. But not everyone will share in it; not all will be able to call it *theirs*. That glory is for those who choose the cross, for those who willingly take it up. And that brings us to a question: Have you taken up the cross? Are you willing to do so?

For if you make the cross yours, this unimaginable glory *will* be yours: A glory that starts here and now when we take up the cross, and which just keeps shining brighter and brighter on into eternity.

1. John R. Claypool, *The Preaching Event* (Waco, TX: Word Books, 1980), p. 64.

2. Ibid., pp. 68-69.

3. Vera Phillips and Edwin Robertson, *J.B. Phillips: The Wounded Healer* (Wm. B. Eerdmans, 1985), pp. 10-11.

4. Ibid., pp. 84, 85.

5. Clyde S. Kilby, ed., from "Transposition" in *A Mind Awake: An Anthology of* C.S. *Lewis* (New York: Harcourt, Brace, Jovanovich, 1969), pp. 167-68.